"Jan Johnson has a particular ar
with the living God through]
exercises have been invaluabl

Christian Spiritual Formation, anu it s exciting to see her guides become more widely available. *Meeting God in Scripture* is a real gift for any of us who desire to spend more time with—and deepen our friendship with—the triune God."

Carolyn Arends, director of education, Renovaré

"Jan does something few contemporary lectio guides do: she preserves the discipline of study that was part of the ancient tradition of lectio divina by providing historical and cultural background for the chosen texts. Her selection of passages is nothing short of brilliant—theologically central, experientially deep, and comprehensively transformational. This guide can be the spark that causes the Word of God to be a fire in your bones once again."

Howard Baker, assistant professor of Christian formation, Denver Seminary

"In her writing as in person, Jan Johnson finds ordinary ways to guide us into extraordinary experiences—into the very presence of God—with an attentive ear for what God may have to say. What a personal yet practical way to bring the practice of lectio divina into daily life! The coaching Jan provides is spot-on soul guidance and will most certainly help readers greatly increase their capacity for meeting God in Scripture."

Mindy Caliguire, founder, Soul Care

"Finally, a book about engaging Scripture for personal and group transformation has arrived! Jan Johnson has done a great service for evangelicals who have lost an imagination for reading the Bible outside of study or quick inspiration. *Meeting God in Scripture* is a beautiful reclaiming of lectio divina for our time. Read, ponder, pray, and meditate on the beauty of Scripture as described in these pages and prepare to be changed!"

Keith J. Matthews, professor of spiritual formation and leadership, Azusa Pacific

"What a great title—and what a great book! God delights to meet with his children in Scripture, and if you're ready to try out a different approach, let Jan Johnson, an experienced and trusted Bible teacher, lead the way with this sound and practical guide. You'll have the opportunity to meditate on thematically arranged passages from various sections of the whole Bible. I really appreciated the just-enough background comments that helped illuminate key words or concepts so that I could put aside immediate questions and enter more fully into the passage. The structured framework and thoughtful questions prodded my pondering to allow God's work in my heart. This guidebook offers nourishing soul food for those with little or much experience in Bible meditation, individually or in a group setting."

Klaus Issler, author of *Living into the Life of Jesus*

"What a great help! Jan is truly a thoughtful and trusted guide. I love the way this book is laid out and the overarching direction it takes us in. Carefully working through this book will change your life."

Nathan Foster, Renovaré, author of *The Making of an Ordinary Saint*

"I've found encountering God in Scripture to be my favorite and most life-giving spiritual practice. In *Meeting God in Scripture*, Jan serves us as a seasoned guide to the classic spiritual practice of lectio divina through these forty well-crafted and inviting meditations. More than an idea book, this is an experience book. I hope you'll read it and grow in your enjoyment of God in Scripture."

Alan Fadling, president and founder, Unhurried Living, author of *An Unhurried Life*

"Jesus spoke of the wise disciple who 'brings out of his storeroom new treasures as well as old,' and this book does just that. It helps the follower of Jesus practice the call of Scripture to be people who meditate frequently on God's truth. The guidance given here is both time-tested by respected ancient writers and practice-tested in everyday life, as this book has grown out of years of fruitful Bible study leadership. There is a thoughtful grounding of the prayer and meditation exercises in the historical meaning of the text."

James C. Wilhoit, professor of core studies, Scripture Press Professor of Christian Education, Wheaton College

"Jan Johnson has written a wonderful and clear guide to lectio divina. . . . [It] will be of tremendous help to everyone desiring to know God more deeply and to become more like Jesus."

Siang-Yang Tan, professor of psychology, Fuller Theological Seminary, author of *Counseling and Psychotherapy*

"When we experience abandonment, we look for guideposts to bring about renewal. These Scripture meditation exercises invite us into the presence of God, who creates a safe place for us and draws us into a culture for formation and growth."

Glandion Carney, author of *The Way of Grace*

MEETING
GOD
IN SCRIPTURE

A HANDS-ON GUIDE TO
LECTIO DIVINA

Jan Johnson

IVP Books

An imprint of InterVarsity Press
Downers Grove, Illinois

InterVarsity Press
P.O. Box 1400, Downers Grove, IL 60515-1426
ivpress.com
email@ivpress.com

*InterVarsity Press® is the book-publishing division of InterVarsity Christian Fellowship/USA®, a
movement of students and faculty active on campus at hundreds of universities, colleges and schools
of nursing in the United States of America, and a member movement of the International Fellowship
of Evangelical Students. For information about local and regional activities, visit intervarsity.org.*

*All Scripture quotations, unless otherwise indicated, are taken from THE HOLY BIBLE, NEW
INTERNATIONAL VERSION®, NIV® Copyright © 1973, 1978, 1984, 2011 by Biblica, Inc.™ Used by
permission. All rights reserved worldwide.*

*While any stories in this book are true, some names and identifying information may have been
changed to protect the privacy of individuals.*

Cover design: Cindy Kiple
Interior design: Beth McGill
Images: © Christine Amat/Trevillion Images

ISBN 978-0-8308-4622-1 (print)
ISBN 978-0-8308-7331-9 (digital)

Printed in the United States of America ∞

Library of Congress Cataloging-in-Publication Data
A catalog record for this book is available from the Library of Congress.

P	25	24	23	22	21	20	19	18	17	16	15	14	13	12	11	10	9	8	7	6	5	4	3	2	1
Y	34	33	32	31	30	29	28	27	26	25	24	23	22	21	20	19	18	17	16						

To the thousands of students and retreat participants

who tried these meditation exercises, met God in the midst

and stunned me with what came to them

Contents

Introduction

I've been leading groups of people in meditating on Scripture for twenty years, helping them enter into the biblical text, notice what resonates with them and then reflect on that. People tell me they get a sense of hearing God speak to them in the group setting, but they struggle to do the same type of study and meditation on their own. The historical and cultural background I provide helps them, and I help them picture details of the scene for narrative passages. People seem to focus better when I ask them questions to guide them through the process of meditation.

This book does all those things, coming alongside to help people interact with the Holy Spirit as they meditate on Scripture passages.

Each session provides

- an introductory space of silence to help you relax and refocus, and an optional question or exercise if you need more help in settling in;
- the full text of a Scripture passage with explanations of unusual or important words;
- meanings of some important words in Hebrew or Greek (including the reference numbers for *Strong's Hebrew and Greek Dictionary*);
- questions to help you enter the text;
- questions about what resonates with you in the text, discerning what God's invitation might be (this is the lectio divina approach: read, reflect, respond, rest);

- cultural or historical background as needed;
- connections with other Scripture as needed;
- cues to help you picture how the story unfolds in narrative passages (an Ignatian approach);
- space to respond to God in prayer;
- space to prayerfully contemplate the ideas of the passage and the person of God; and
- an exercise to "try on" one of the main ideas of the passage later.

You may wonder whether all these helps might somehow interfere with or obscure what the Spirit is saying to you. I wondered the same thing myself, even though most people find that the helps clarify what the Spirit is saying. So I conferred with others who are well-practiced in leading Scripture meditation. They agreed that many Christians want to do this type of spiritual exercise but need some direction. One colleague urged me to write this book to provide "training wheels" to help people move into Scripture meditation.

USING THIS BOOK ON YOUR OWN

You may use the forty meditation exercises in this book in any order you wish. They are organized by topic to help you choose the meditations that will best meet your needs. The eight sections address needs that most people experience. For example, I began meditating on Scripture many years ago because I sensed I had a "delight deficiency." I did not *truly believe* that God delighted in me, so I meditated on passages that addressed that issue (see the meditation in this book titled "Knowing I Am Loved").

When attempting any spiritual practice, it's wise to consider how the Christian community throughout history has done it so that we can learn from them. For example, when you want to study a passage, you might have a look at Bible studies or commentaries that other Christians have written about the passage at different times and places.

At least since the fifth century, one of the primary ways Christians have meditated on Scripture is by reading a passage and then following the Jewish idea of "taking hold" and "keeping" God's words (Proverbs 4:3-4). Christians began calling this process lectio divina, which is a Latin phrase for "divine reading" or "sacred reading" (from ecclesiastical Latin, pronounced *LEX-ee-oh dih-VEE-nuh*). The central idea of lectio divina is *invitation*. Lectio divina assumes that God is inviting us into interaction and conversation as we read Scripture.

There are four traditional steps in lectio divina—Read (*lectio*), Reflect (*meditatio*), Respond (*oratio*) and Rest (*contemplatio*). For these meditations I've added two more: Relax and Refocus (*silencio*), and Trying It On (*incarnatio*).[1]

***Relax and refocus* (silencio).** Each exercise begins with brief guidance to slow down, quiet your inner self and let go of distracting thoughts. This is important because most people spend all day responding to stimuli—answering the telephone, following schedules and evaluating what needs to be done next. Even when they wake up the first thing they do is check their phone for messages. So when they try to meditate on Scripture, these activities become traffic in their heads that keep them from focusing on God.

A way to interrupt this traffic is to focus on being present in the moment by breathing in and out deeply—even overbreathing. It also helps to relax our body parts one by one: bending the neck, letting the arms go limp, relaxing the legs and ankles. Loosen each part from the inside out. This doesn't mean you're setting aside your mind—you're redirecting your mind away from the busyness that often consumes you. Being present in the moment prepares you to wait on the still, small voice of God.

If you are distracted, you may want to try the palms up, palms down method. Rest your hands in your lap, placing your hands palms down as a symbol of turning over any concerns you have. If a nagging thought arises, turn your hands palms up as a "symbol of your desire to receive from the Lord."[2] If you become distracted at any time during meditation, repeat the exercise.

If you are new to Scripture meditation, a focus question or activity is provided to help you quiet yourself and let go of distractions. As you become more skilled at Scripture meditation you may not need to do this, or you may find that option intrusive, as if the instructions are circumventing something that the Spirit might suggest. In that case, feel free to skip this option.

You may want to develop your own simple "relax and refocus" practice to use each time. Singing a favorite song may be helpful—especially a quiet one, such as the old hymn "Spirit of the Living God, Fall Fresh on Me." Or you may want to read a good quote, such as this one from Dietrich Bonhoeffer. Say it aloud, slowly.

> In our meditation we ponder the chosen text on the strength of the promise that it has something utterly personal to say to us today and for our Christian life. . . . We read God's Word as God's Word for us.[3]

*Read (*lectio*).* In these meditations I will often ask you to read the passage aloud, and to read it a few times. That's because the first time we read a passage, we barely absorb what's going on. Reading aloud allows the words to "fall on our ear" and increases our perception of what is said. Listen slowly to each word with the "ear of your heart," so to speak. Be open and attentive to whatever stands out to you.

*Reflect (*meditatio*).* Some of the passages in this book are teaching or discourse passages. You are invited to notice what stands out or "shimmers" for you, trusting that this is the prompting of the Holy Spirit. Other passages are stories. Here you are invited to use your imagination to picture the scene using the cues provided. In both cases, the background information and questions will help you immerse yourself in the passage and set aside distractions.

With narrative passages, the questions and cues will help ground you in a concrete way—what are you seeing or smelling?—but don't try too hard to create a careful, detailed picture. Your goal is to let God speak to you, not to do a perfect reconstruction of the event. Establish yourself in the setting and then move through the passage to let God speak to you.

Sometimes much of the scene will elude you, but a particular word or image will stand out. In the story of the woman with the issue of blood (Mark 5:24-34), I was struck once by the words "whole truth," which she told Jesus. I felt her embarrassment as she spoke out. I saw her being publicly vulnerable to Jesus, the prophet, and it made me see just how real I could be with God.

*Respond (*oratio*).* A truly interactive life with God will be one in which God speaks to you (most often through Scripture) and where you respond to God about what you think you have heard. You may wish to ask God questions at this time or even protest what has come to you. If nothing else, you may wish to thank God for speaking to you through Scripture.

*Rest (*contemplatio*).* This last phase step provides space to simply be present with God. You can contemplate what has come to you, or to absorb the flow of the conversation with God, or to notice how the interaction affected you. You may also find yourself worshiping God who says and does marvelous things.

*Trying it on (*incarnatio*).* Finally, in each meditation I offer a brief suggestion to invite you to take some action that embodies a truth in the passage. If the suggestion doesn't resonate with you, ask God to show you a different way to experiment with living out something from the passage, even in a small way.

Throughout this book you will find call-out boxes that provide information and guidance about how to meditate on Scripture, or that answer frequently asked questions. You may read them all in one sitting or as you move through the book.

The goal of this book is to help you interact with God through Scripture in a formative way. As Dallas Willard writes,

> I find myself addressed, caught up in all the individuality of my concrete existence by something beyond me. God acts toward me in a distinctively personal manner. This is the common testimony across wide ranges of Christian fellowship and history. . . . We stand within a community of the spoken to.[4]

Using This Book with a Group

The book addresses readers as individuals, but it can easily be used in groups with a few modifications. Groups of no more than four or five work best, but if you have more, divide into groups of no more than four or five with one person leading each. The meditation exercises may be led by anyone by simply following the directions, but here are some things to think about.

Relax and refocus (**silencio**). The group may wish to decide beforehand if they want to use the optional exercises. If they are used, the group leader can read the instructions aloud and participants can speak their responses aloud to the group. Some group members may not wish to share their answers or may not have a response. While verbal answers usually help the others in the group, passing on a response is always allowed.

If the group prefers, they may wish to use a favorite prayer as an opening relax and refocus exercise. They may even wish to use it every time, so that it develops into a comfortable way to settle in.

Here is one possibility. Participants may read this aloud together:

> Let us release the cares of our day,
> and open our eyes to the wonder of God.
> With an attitude of empathy to people of another time,
> let us open our hearts and minds to God.

Let us prepare to experience God's Word to us through the presence of the Holy Spirit.[5]

Or,

May the words of our mouths and the meditations of our heart be acceptable in your sight, O Lord, our Strength and our Redeemer.

Read (lectio). The leader will read the instructions and then the passage aloud the first time, slowly. Participants may wish to close their eyes to listen, or to follow along in the book. The leader should ask another participant to read the notes below the text aloud. Then either the leader or someone else should read the passage again.

Reflect (meditatio). Participants will read the questions and cues silently and take a few minutes to write down their responses to the questions. Then the leader may read each question aloud and those who are willing can share their answers. Background statements may be read aloud also.

This sort of meditative exercise is not a discussion, however. Commenting on other participants' answers may be distracting. The point is to listen to God in Scripture, not to talk about it with others. If someone is troubled or puzzled by the passage, it's not a good idea to immediately address this. The process allows quiet moments for the Spirit to do that. The purpose is not so much analysis (although that does occur), but to listen to God and to learn to be truly present to each other as group members describe their experiences.

The leader asks someone to read the passage aloud again. Then the leader may read the questions listed in that section, allowing a few minutes after each one for participants to consider their answers silently. Those willing to share can do so after time is given to consider the answer.

Again, this is not a discussion group, but participants are telling others what they believe God might be saying to them. It's wise not to evaluate what others say, as this usually prevents people from hearing God for themselves. It's equally important that participants don't interrupt each other or make suggestions. Instead, trust the Spirit to illuminate the Word to each person. Frequently, participants understand more as they try to put their experience into their own words.

Respond (oratio). Normal conversation involves back and forth. Since God speaks to us in Scripture, participants need to reply back to God. Some participants may wish to read their prayers aloud, while others will not.

Whatever is spoken or written needs to address God, as in prayer, not the group. The prayer concerns what participants most want to say to God about their experience in the Scripture passage.

Participants may want to ask God questions. The answers to these questions may come through the group or to the individuals later in the week. Writing prayers down can be a powerful way of communicating with God, and at the very least can keep the mind from wandering.

Rest (contemplatio). Participants will most likely wish to do this in silence. However, it's also possible that a participant will wish to reflect aloud on how God seemed during this time of meditation. Did God seem to be present to you? If so, what was that like to you?

Trying it on (incarnatio). The group leader should read this suggestion aloud and ask the other participants to consider whether it fits with their own conversations with God. They may wish to modify it, do something else or do nothing.

A NOTE ABOUT QUIET

This format involves a lot of quiet, and some people find being quiet in a group difficult. In most groups, people talk a lot! This version of group lectio divina provides a different kind of togetherness. A sense of community can be developed without small talk or chitchat. It helps to use fewer words, offering only the words and images that resonate within you.

As stated above, sometimes participants are unable to verbalize their answers or are unwilling to share with the group something that is too personal. It's fine to pass. For some participants, sitting in the quiet is a little difficult and they may wish to doodle in the margin of their book. Others may find the quietness refreshing because they don't have to come up with something to say. The quiet actually provides the space to hear God more easily.

USING THIS BOOK WITH SPECIFIC GROUPS

Scripture meditation is not only for those already familiar with Scripture. The meditative approach of this book works well with many ages, including children and teens, and with adults in many situations, although modifications will need to be made. This means taking into account more limited attention spans and reworking or omitting ideas that might not be easily understood. If you usually teach in a specific setting, such as in prisons or among the homeless, you'll already have some idea what modifications need to be made.

With all kinds of groups, it works well to meditate on a narrative passage by reading and studying it first, and then acting it out—even with adults. If you do this, pause ("freeze-frame") at certain moments in the action of the passage and ask participants to assume the role of certain characters. Then you might ask, "How do you feel about what is happening?" Ask, "What kind of look (would you suppose) is on Jesus' face based on the text and the cues provided?" This can create some riveting moments of encountering Christ as never before.

Why Meditate on Scripture?

Meditation on Scripture was a common activity in Jewish culture. It is mentioned fifteen times just in the Psalms.[1] Those who meditated on the law day and night flourished like trees planted by streams of water. Meditating on Scripture gave the psalmists wisdom that surpassed their teachers and enemies, led to diligent obedience and kept them out of temptation's way. Meditation was a delightful practice—God's words tasted sweeter than honey (Psalm 1:1-3; 119:97-103).

Scripture meditation has been so neglected in the last century that some have come to associate meditation only with Eastern religions. But the fact that meditation is common in Eastern religions doesn't mean it is wrong. Eastern religions practice other disciplines Christians practice, such as fasting, praying and even repeating quotations from Jesus. Perhaps Scripture meditation became infrequent because of the post-Enlightenment emphasis on science and linear thinking, which displaced reflection and rest (two ideas found prominently in the Psalms).

*Like all spiritual disciplines, Scripture meditation is another way to become more attentive to the still, small voice of God and to become more willing to respond when we hear it. Paired with the study of Scripture, meditation helps both those who are new to faith and those who feel like they've heard it all before. Even if you're familiar with the words and ideas, in Scripture meditation God speaks the words we need to hear in our life today. Because meditating on Scripture helps us hear God's Word **to us**, we experience even well-known passages in fresh ways.*

Knowing God as Love

1 Corinthians 13:4-8

RELAX AND REFOCUS (*SILENCIO*)

Center yourself by breathing slowly in and out. Relax your neck and take time to let your muscles relax.

If a distraction interrupts you (such as remembering something you need to do), rest your hands in your lap with your palms up and offer that distraction to God. Turn your hands over to signify receiving God's peace.

Optional—You may wish to begin by considering this question: When have I felt truly loved?

READ (*LECTIO*)

Read the passage to yourself silently. As you read, do not concern yourself with how your life measures up to what love is. This passage isn't about the kind of love that humans typically exhibit, but about *agapē* love, which is engaging the will for the good of another.[1] Paul is describing divine love here.

1 Corinthians 13:4-8

⁴Love is patient, love is kind. It does not envy, it does not boast, it is not proud. ⁵It does not dishonor others, it is not self-seeking, it is not easily angered, it keeps no record of wrongs. ⁶Love does not delight in evil but rejoices with the truth. ⁷It always protects, always trusts, always hopes, always perseveres.

⁸Love never fails.

Because Paul was writing about divine love, it may help to substitute the word *God* for *love*. As the apostle John wrote, "We know and rely on the love God has for us. God is love. Whoever lives in love lives in God, and God in them" (1 John 4:16). We may infer, then, that whatever love is like, God is also like.

Read the passage aloud a second time, substituting the word *God* for *love*:

⁴God is patient, God is kind. He God does not envy, does not boast, is not proud. ⁵He does not dishonor others, is not self-seeking, is not easily angered, keeps no record of wrongs. ⁶God does not delight in evil but rejoices with the truth. ⁷He always protects, always trusts, always hopes, always perseveres. ⁸God never fails.

REFLECT (*MEDITATIO*)

Questions and cues to help you reflect on the passage.

1. Which qualities or actions from the passage surprise you when they are attributed to God? Why do you think that surprises you?

2. Consider these versions of 1 Corinthians 13:4-8. The word *God* has been substituted for *love* and a few adaptations have been made.

Which descriptions of God do you find most engaging? Most disturbing? Most surprising?

NRSV	N. T. Wright translation*	*The Message*
God is patient	God is great-hearted	God never gives up
God is kind	kind	God cares more for others than for self
God is not envious	knows no jealousy	God doesn't want what [he] doesn't have
or boastful	makes no fuss	God doesn't strut
or arrogant	is not puffed up	doesn't have a swelled head
or rude	knows no shameful ways	doesn't force [his] own self on others
God does not insist on [his] own way	doesn't force rightful claims	isn't always "me first"
not irritable	doesn't rage	doesn't fly off the handle
or resentful	doesn't bear a grudge	doesn't keep score of the sins of others
does not rejoice in wrongdoing	doesn't cheer at others' harm	doesn't revel when others grovel
rejoices in the truth	rejoices in the truth	takes pleasure in the flowering of truth
bears all things	bears all things	puts up with anything
believes all things	believes all things	trusts always
hopes all things	hopes all things	always looks for the best
endures all things	endures all things	never looks back
God never ends	God never fails	keeps going to the end
*Tom Wright, Paul for Everyone: 1 Corinthians (Louisville, KY: Westminster John Knox Press, 2004), 175.		

3. What Scripture passages or stories come to mind that bear out the truth that God is love? For example, consider Israel's behavior from the exodus through the judges, the monarchy, the divided kingdom, the dispersion and Judah's return from Persia. God's persistent love, despite Israel's tendency to depend on other gods and on themselves, shows us that God never gives up.

4. *Setting cue: Paul's point of view.* Picture the apostle Paul writing to the Corinthian church he knew so well, and realizing that "there are quarrels among you" (1 Corinthians 1:11). Even in the early church,

love could be forgotten in the midst of controversy. As N. T. Wright says, "People sometimes talk as if first-generation Christianity enjoyed a pure, untroubled honeymoon period, after which things became more difficult; but there is no evidence for this in the New Testament."[2] Paul painted a picture of living life with God's kind of love.

Perhaps Paul was in tears because of their quarrels as he wrote these words. Or he may have been captivated by a majestic, penetrating view of God.

Reflect on the invitation. Perhaps God is offering you an invitation through this passage to enlarge your understanding or to think and feel differently about what God is like. Read the passage again and then sit quietly for a few minutes, pondering these questions:

- What words or phrases stand out to you?
- Why do you think that is?

Reflect a little further. You may wish to read the passage again. Then consider:

- How does this passage connect with your life?
- Is there some idea, feeling or intention you need to embrace from it? If so, what?
- What might God be inviting you to be, know, understand, feel or do?

Be open to the quiet, and don't feel pressured to come up with an answer.

RESPOND (*ORATIO*)

Take a few minutes to respond to God in prayer. What do you most want to say to God about this experience in Scripture?

You may ask God questions (the answers to which may come to you later). You may wish to write your prayer down. Sometimes that helps keep our minds from wandering.

Rest (*CONTEMPLATIO*)

Soak in what has stood out to you and consider your overall impression of God from this passage. Notice how it feels to know you are "fully known" by God, as Paul writes later in the same chapter (verse 12).

Spend a few minutes soaking in the thoughts that have come to you. This may take the form of worship, or of simply resting in God's presence.

Trying It On (*INCARNATIO*)

Read the passage a few times throughout your day or week, pondering how God shows to you the kind of love described in this passage. How is God patient with you? How is God not rude or pushy with you? How does God always protect you?

Sought After, No Matter What

Luke 15:1-7

RELAX AND REFOCUS (*SILENCIO*)

Take a few deep breaths and let go of the thoughts that have occupied your mind.

Optional—If you wish, consider this question to focus your thoughts on today's passage: What does it feel like to be found when you've been lost? Take a few minutes to reflect. It's okay if nothing comes to mind right away. Just enjoy God's presence.

READ (*LECTIO*)

Read the passage to yourself. Then read the notes below it about the key words and phrases. Consider how these details affect your understanding of the story. Then read the passage aloud slowly. Take time to let the words "fall on your ear."

REFLECT (*MEDITATIO*)

Questions and cues to help you enter into the story.

1. Jesus told this parable in response to the criticism of the Pharisees that Jesus ate with tax collectors and "sinners." Contrast the shepherd's behavior with the Pharisees' behavior.

Luke 15:1-7

¹Now the tax collectors and **sinners** were all gathering around to hear Jesus. ²But the Pharisees and the teachers of the law muttered, "This man welcomes sinners and eats with them."

³Then Jesus told them this parable: ⁴"Suppose one of you has a hundred sheep and loses one of them. Doesn't he leave the ninety-nine in the open country and go after the lost sheep until he finds it? ⁵And when he finds it, he joyfully puts it on his shoulders ⁶and goes home. Then he calls his friends and neighbors together and says, 'Rejoice with me; I have found my lost sheep.' ⁷I tell you that in the same way there will be more rejoicing in heaven over one sinner who repents than over **ninety-nine righteous persons who do not need to repent.**"

---

sinners The tax collectors and sinners were the lowest stratum of society, while Pharisees were among the highest.[1] The Pharisees considered the people of the land "sinners" because they didn't keep the law in great detail.[2]

ninety-nine righteous persons who do not need to repent Jesus compared the ninety-nine sheep to people who thought they didn't need to repent. Like the older son in the prodigal son parable, they didn't think they had a problem.[3]

The Pharisees were eager to:

The shepherd was eager to:

2. Underline phrases in the text that show the eagerness and enthusiasm of the shepherd, such as "go after the lost sheep" (verse 4).

3. *Cultural background: "Leave the ninety-nine in the open country" (verse 4).* Instead of following the custom of securing the sheep in a sheepfold or leaving them under the care of another shepherd, the shepherd in this story did neither. This must have mystified hearers. Why would the shepherd do such a thing? Perhaps Jesus intended for the rash behavior of the shepherd to underscore the theme that God pursues each person madly and passionately. If so, this story

would have been a shocking rejoinder to the Pharisees, who didn't like the fact that Jesus was associating with sinners (verse 3), or the idea that God would go out of his way to draw sinners to faith.

4. *Cultural background: The heart of the shepherd.* Sheepherder Phillip Keller, who has spent many hours searching for lost sheep, explains that if a shepherd doesn't arrive in time to rescue a "cast" sheep, it could die. Lying on its back, its feet in the air, frantically struggling to stand up, the sheep feels gases build up in its belly and its blood circulation is cut off. It cannot right itself. "This is another reason why it is essential for a careful sheepman to look over his flock every day. If one or two are missing, often the first thought to flash into the shepherd's mind is, *One of my sheep is cast somewhere. I must go in search and set it on its feet again.*"[4]

In what situation do you wish God would find you, and restore you to tranquility?

5. *Fly on the wall cue: Picture the lost sheep.* Picture how a lost sheep would have responded to hearing the familiar call of its shepherd. (Shepherds usually have a distinct call.) Sheep recognize their shepherd's call instantly and obey because they've learned the voice that guides them to their watering place every day, whose staff untangles them from brambles and wild roses, whose voice brings them to shelter before a storm hits.

Reflect on the invitation. Read the passage again and picture what the scene might look like as if you were watching a movie. Hear the words clearly in your mind.

- As you watch the action unfold, what do you see?
- What moment in the story, or what word or phrase stands out to you? What does this cause you to think and feel?
- Why do you think that is? What significance might this have for you?

Reflect a little further.

- How does this passage connect with your life?
- Is there some idea, feeling or intention you need to embrace from it? If so, what?
- What might God be inviting you to be, know, understand, feel or do?

Be open to the quiet and don't feel pressured to come up with an answer.

RESPOND (*ORATIO*)

Take a few minutes to respond to God about this in prayer. You may wish to ask God questions.

If you're willing, write your prayer, beginning with, Dear God, . . . Then consider, What do you most want to say to God about this experience in Scripture?

REST (*CONTEMPLATIO*)

Soak in whatever stood out to you in this passage. If something stood out to you in particular, absorb that more fully. Perhaps you want to soak in the feeling of being found and cherished by God.

TRYING IT ON (*INCARNATIO*)

Later today or tomorrow, put something on your shoulders—a board or even a towel. Notice how close to your eyes and mouth this object is, just as the sheep would have been very close to the shepherd's face when the shepherd turned to look at it on his shoulders. Consider what this would have been like for a sheep to be held so tightly by the shepherd. What might Jesus have wanted to convey about our relationship with God by using this imagery?

Knowing I Am Loved

Isaiah 43:1-7

RELAX AND REFOCUS (*SILENCIO*)

Inhale and exhale a few times. Let go of distractions. You may wish to lie on the floor on your back, put your feet up and open your palms toward the sky or ceiling. Quiet your thoughts and open yourself to God. Prepare to experience God's Word to us through the presence of the Holy Spirit.

Optional—Consider this question: What does it feel like to know you truly belong?

READ (*LECTIO*)

Read the passage to yourself silently. Then read the notes below it about the key words and phrases. Consider how these details help your understanding of the passage. Then read the passage aloud, slowly. Take time to let the words "fall on your ear."

REFLECT (*MEDITATIO*)

Questions and cues to help you reflect on the passage.

1. Twice God urged the people of Judah not to be afraid. What reasons does God give for this?

Isaiah 43:1-7

¹But now, this is **what the LORD says**—
  he who created you, Jacob,
  he who formed you, Israel:
"Do not fear, for I have redeemed you;
  I have summoned you by name;
    you are mine.
²When you pass through the waters,
  I will be with you;
and when you pass through the rivers,
  they will not sweep over you.
When you walk through the fire,
  you will not be burned;
  the flames will not set you ablaze.
³For I am the LORD your God,
  the Holy One of Israel, your Savior;
I give Egypt for your **ransom**,
  Cush and Seba in your stead.
⁴Since you are precious and honored in my sight,
  and because I love you,
I will give people in exchange for you,
  nations in exchange for your life.
⁵Do not be afraid, for I am with you;
  I will bring your children **from the east**
  and gather you from the west.

what the LORD says Old Testament poetry and prophecy are often interrupted by the surprising speech of God. It's as if we are invited to stand at attention in those moments.
you are mine God dotes like this even over disobedient Israel (as described in Isaiah 42:22-25). God shows mercy and restores spiritual failures.
ransom Persia conquered Egypt, Cush and Seba, but released Judah.
from the east Judah had been carried off into captivity by Babylon, but God delivered them and brought them back.

> **⁶**I will say to the north, 'Give them up!'
>   and to the south, 'Do not hold them back.'
> Bring my sons from afar
>   and my daughters from the ends of the earth—
> **⁷**everyone who is called by my name,
>   whom I created for my glory,
> whom I formed and made."

2. Of the ideas offered in this passage (some of which are listed here), which ones are most significant for you today?

- God formed us (verses 1, 7)
- God redeems us—bringing us back from sin and despair (verses 1, 5, 6)
- God walks with us through sweeping rivers of water and empowers us to walk through flames without being burned (verse 2)
- God is the Lord *our* God (verse 3)
- God has paid a hefty ransom for us (verses 3, 4)
- God views us as precious and honored (verse 4)
- God loves us (verse 4)
- God is with us (verse 5)
- God created us to glorify himself (verse 7)

Read the passage aloud again. Consider verses 2-7 coming from the mind of God to you in a special way.

Reflect on the invitation. Read the passage again, and ask yourself these questions:

- What word or phrase stands out to you?
- Why do you think that is?

Reflect a little further. Perhaps God is offering you an invitation in this passage to enlarge your understanding about something. What might that be? Read the passage again and then sit quietly for a few minutes, pondering these questions:

- How does this passage connect with your life?
- Is there some idea, feeling or intention you need to embrace from it? If so, what?
- What might God be inviting you to be, know, understand, feel or do?

Be open to the quiet, and don't feel pressured to come up with an answer.

RESPOND (*ORATIO*)

Repeat back to God whatever word or phrase stuck out to you from the passage, and tell God how that word or phrase connects with your life today. Bring whatever requests you might have based on this. Tell God about your response to this—are you puzzled? Doubtful? Amazed?

REST (*CONTEMPLATIO*)

Soak in the idea that *you belong*. You belong to the one who really matters. How does that feel?

TRYING IT ON (*INCARNATIO*)

Many songs are based on this passage. Find a song that resonates with you.

God's Compassion
for the Rebellious

Luke 15:11-24

RELAX AND REFOCUS (*SILENCIO*)

Center yourself by breathing slowly in and out. Relax your neck and breathe out again. Let your shoulders relax.

Optional—You may wish to begin by considering a sentence that I once saw on a coffee mug: *God is crazy about you—and there's nothing you can do about it.* At first I thought it was a little frivolous. But by the next day, I started saying it to myself, because I'm convinced that it's something most people don't really believe.

How does that phrase strike you? How likely is it that God is *crazy about you*, and not merely tolerating you?

READ (*LECTIO*)

Read the passage to yourself. Then read the notes below it about the key words and phrases. Consider how these details affect your understanding of the story. Then read the passage aloud slowly. Take time to let the words "fall on your ear."

Luke 15:11-24

11Jesus continued: "There was a man who had two sons. **12**The younger one said to his father, 'Father, *give me my share of the estate.*' So he divided his property between them.

13"Not long after that, the younger son got together all he had, set off for a distant country and there squandered his wealth in wild living. **14**After he had spent everything, there was a severe famine in that whole country, and he began to be in need. **15**So he went and hired himself out to a citizen of that country, who sent him to his fields to *feed pigs*. **16**He longed to fill his stomach with the pods that the pigs were eating, but no one gave him anything.

17"When he came to his senses, he said, 'How many of my father's hired servants have food to spare, and here I am starving to death! **18**I will set out and go back to my father and say to him: Father, I have sinned against heaven and against you. **19**I am no longer worthy to be called your son; make me like one of your hired servants.' **20**So he got up and went to his father.

"But while he was still a long way off, his father saw him and was filled with compassion for him; he *ran to his son*, threw his arms around him and kissed him.

21"The son said to him, 'Father, I have sinned against heaven and against you. I am no longer worthy to be called your son.'

---

give me my share of the estate It was as if the son had said, "Let's pretend you're dead. I'll take my half now." This disrespectful behavior would have been shocking to Jesus' listeners—perhaps even worthy of stoning. Striking or cursing parents brought a penalty of death (Exodus 21:15, 17). A stubborn or rebellious child could be stoned (Deuteronomy 21:18-21).

feed pigs If he was feeding pigs (and possibly eating the pigs' food), the young man was not living an approved Jewish lifestyle, since pigs were unclean in Jewish culture (Deuteronomy 14:8-10). That would have made him a social outcast. He may have been shunned by the Jewish community.

ran to his son "Middle Eastern adult men [did] not run in public if they wished to avoid public shame. The father exposed himself to public humiliation."[1]

robe, ring, sandals, party The father met the son's needs by offering him honor (a robe and sandals), authority (the signet ring) and a party (killing the fattened calf).

> ²²"But the father said to his servants, 'Quick! Bring the best **robe** and put it on him. Put a **ring** on his finger and **sandals** on his feet. ²³Bring the fattened calf and kill it. Let's have a feast and celebrate. ²⁴For this son of mine was dead and is alive again; he was lost and is found.' So they began to celebrate."

REFLECT (*MEDITATIO*)

Questions and cues to help you enter into the story.

1. Which of the father's behaviors do you find most intriguing?

   - That he didn't refuse to grant the son's request
   - That he was so attentive to the son's absence that he spotted the son while he was still far away
   - That he spoke before the son could confess what he had done wrong
   - That he gave this returning son honor and authority after the son had proved he didn't deserve it
   - Other:_____

2. What word would you use to describe the father's behavior? Selfless? Eager? Lavish?

3. *Fly on the wall cue: Picture the clothing.* As the boy headed home, he probably wore a tattered coarse garment such as swineherds customarily wore. His father offered him more than the conventional outer cloak: he put a long flowing elaborate garment, or stole, on him—the same garment inhabitants of heaven will wear (Revelation 6:11).[2]

   Reflect on the invitation. Read the passage aloud again. Picture what the scene would look like. Hear the words clearly.

- As you watch the action unfold, what do you see?

- What moment in the story, or what word or phrase stands out to you? What does this make you think and feel?

- Why do you think that is? What significance might this have for you? *Reflect a little further.*

- Is God perhaps inviting you to reconsider your view of him? Or of yourself? Or of the way relationship with God works?

- Is there any idea, feeling or intention you need to embrace from this story? If so, what?

Be open to the quiet and don't feel pressured to come up with an answer.

RESPOND (*ORATIO*)

Take a few minutes to respond to God about this in prayer. What do you most want to say to God about what you saw or heard in this passage?

Consider writing your prayer down so that your thoughts will be as clear as possible.

REST (*CONTEMPLATIO*)

Revisit the excitement of the father running down the road to embrace his son. Sense how this represents God's excitement at being reunited with you. Rest in that thought and the feelings that go with it.

TRYING IT ON (*INCARNATIO*)

Consider the phrase referenced above: *God is crazy about you—and there's nothing you can do about it.* Ask God to show you a person or two who might benefit from hearing that said to them. If you're willing, say it to them.

5

God's Compassion
for the Outwardly Compliant

Luke 15:25-32

RELAX AND REFOCUS (*SILENCIO*)

Inhale and exhale a few times. Let go of any distractions. Quiet your thoughts and open yourself to God.

Optional—If you wish, use this little exercise to help you focus: "Imagine God thinking about you. What do you assume God feels when you come to mind?"[1]

READ (*LECTIO*)

Read the passage to yourself. Then read the notes below it about the key words and phrases. Consider how these details affect your understanding of the story. Then read the passage aloud slowly. Take time to let the words "fall on your ear."

REFLECT (*MEDITATIO*)

Questions and cues to help you enter into the story.

1. The older son had missed the point! Even though he obeyed his father and did what was right, he related to his father as a slave-master, not as a father. While the younger son wasted the father's

Luke 15:25-32

²⁵"Meanwhile, the older son was in the field. When he came near the house, he heard music and dancing. ²⁶So he called one of the servants and asked him what was going on. ²⁷'Your brother has come,' he replied, 'and your father has killed the fattened calf because he has him back safe and sound.'

²⁸"The *older brother* became angry and refused to go in. So his *father went out and pleaded* with him. ²⁹But he answered his father, 'Look! All these years I've been *slaving* for you and never disobeyed your orders. Yet you never gave me even a young goat so I could celebrate with my friends. ³⁰But when this *son of yours* who has squandered your property with prostitutes comes home, you kill the fattened calf for him!'

³¹"'My son,' the father said, 'you are always with me, and everything I have is yours. ³²But we had to celebrate and be glad, because this *brother of yours* was dead and is alive again; he was lost and is found.'"

---

older brother The older brother is responding to the news that his rebellious younger brother has returned home and is being welcomed with acceptance and even honor.

father went out and pleaded The father's dignity is compromised again, just as it was when he ran out to greet his younger, wayward son. Now he comes out to meet his older son too.

slaving Working hard with no wages or little reward and without a personal or familial relationship to the master.

son of yours The older son dismisses his relationship with his brother and associates the "problem son" only with the father.

brother of yours The father reminds the older son of his relationship to his younger brother.

possessions, the older son wasted his father's presence and saw himself as a slave. The older missed out on companionship with his father ("always with me") as well as the delight in his responsibility of working the land and being groomed to take over ("everything I have is yours").

2. People often do the same by focusing on outward behavior and missing out on the daily "dependence upon the hand of God in a 'with God' life."[2] How do you think such a "with God life" is different from our normal day-to-day existence?

3. Notice how inviting the father is. He comes out of the house and pleads with this son, rather than demanding the son come to him. What does this tell you about God?

4. In what circumstance might you need to hear these words from God: "You are always with me, and everything I have is yours"?

5. *Fly on the wall cue: Picture the father going out and and pleading with his son (verse 28).* Once again the father defers to his son rather than the son deferring to the father. Henri Nouwen described it this way:

> All boundaries of patriarchal behavior are broken through. This is not the picture of a remarkable father. This is the portrayal of God, whose goodness, love, forgiveness, care and compassion have no limits at all.[3]

What might have been the look on the father's face as he came out of the house and pleaded with his son?

Reflect on the invitation. Read the passage aloud again. Picture what the scene would look like. Hear the words clearly.

• As you watch the action unfold, what do you see?

• What moment in the story, or what word or phrase stands out to you? What does this cause you to think and feel?

• Why do you think that is? What significance might this have for you?
  Reflect a little further.

• How does this passage connect with your life?

• Is there some idea, feeling or intention you need to embrace from it? If so, what?

• What might God be inviting you to be, know, understand, feel or even do? Be open to the quiet and don't feel pressured to come up with an answer.

RESPOND (*ORATIO*)

Take a few minutes to respond to God in prayer. What do you most want to say to God about this experience in Scripture? Tell God if you think you are missing out on experiences with him, such as companionship or the delightful sense of partnering with him in everyday tasks.

You may wish to ask God questions (the answers to which may come to you through the group or later in the week). You may wish to write your prayer down. Sometimes that keeps our minds from wandering.

REST (*CONTEMPLATIO*)

Soak in whatever has stood out to you in this passage and consider: How did God (or God's actions) seem to you in this passage? What does this tell you about what God is like?

Spend a few minutes soaking in the thoughts that have come to you. This may take the form of worship, or simply resting in God's presence.

TRYING IT ON (*INCARNATIO*)

Be aware of those moments when you are merely going through the motions of life. Pause and imagine God saying to you what the father said to the older son: "You are always with me, and everything I have is yours."

Meditation Is Different from Application

To apply Scripture is to ask oneself, **how does my behavior or thinking compare with the principles of this passage?** *Although this is an excellent question, we often answer it by naming a few of our faults that people have pointed out to us! If we're more open to the Spirit, God may bring to mind a new idea or positive reassurance that fits exactly.*

Scripture meditation resembles application in its process of asking, **how does this passage intersect with my life?** *In Scripture meditation, however, we do not have to come up with a way that the Scripture applies to us. Instead, we wait to get a sense of what God may be saying to us through the Scripture. In other words, we do not initiate this; God does. Nor is it always corrective; often it's something we simply need to be assured of, such as* **I am loved!**

Answers may not come immediately, but the **lectio divina** *process opens us up to an ongoing conversation with God all day in which answers may come from unexpected sources. So application is analysis, not reflection. Discerning an application is a helpful left-brain activity where you connect the dots between the principle of the passage and your life. Meditation is right-brained and intuitive. We let go and listen for what God thinks we need to know.*

The effect of meditation is different too. Instead of feeling pressured to change our behavior, we let the Spirit invite us into a next step. While application may often feel coerced (The passage says X so you **should** *do X), meditation is an invitation (See how Jesus did X? Why don't you try X?)*

Because transformation is as much caught as taught, meditation allows you to "catch" things from the Spirit through the words of Scripture. Meditation then results in a change of character that is unforced and at times seems unplanned. Instead, it is organic.

Scripture meditation goes much deeper than simple application. It opens us up to being completely undone by the Spirit and remade in the presence of the Word of God.

6

Blessed with Every Blessing

Ephesians 1:3-14

RELAX AND REFOCUS (*SILENCIO*)

Center yourself by breathing in and out. Relax your neck and take time to let your muscles relax.

Optional—If you need help to focus, consider a time when you were singled out and chosen to do something you wanted to do. It might be that you were accepted to do a task or something you did was noticed and applauded. What was it? How did you feel about it?

READ (*LECTIO*)

Read the passage silently to yourself. Then read the notes below it about the key words and phrases. Consider how these details help your understanding of the passage. Then read the passage aloud slowly. Take time to let the words "fall on your ear."

REFLECT (*MEDITATIO*)

Questions and cues to help you reflect on the passage.

1. Which of these ideas from the passage would you like to embrace more?

   • God lavishes "every spiritual blessing" on us.

Ephesians 1:3-14 (NRSV)

3Blessed be the God and Father of our Lord Jesus Christ, who has blessed us in Christ with every spiritual blessing in the heavenly places, **4**just as he chose us in Christ before the foundation of the world to be *holy* and blameless before him in love. **5**He *destined* us for *adoption* as his children through Jesus Christ, according to the good pleasure of his will, **6**to the praise of his glorious *grace* that he freely bestowed on us in *the Beloved.*

7In him we have redemption through his blood, the *forgiveness of our trespasses*, according to the riches of his grace **8**that he lavished on us. With all wisdom and insight **9**he has made known to us the mystery of his will, according to his good pleasure that he set forth in Christ, **10**as a plan for the fullness of time, to gather up all things in him, things in heaven and things on earth.

11In Christ we have also obtained an *inheritance*, having been destined according to the purpose of him who accomplishes all things according to his counsel and will, **12**so that we, who were the first to set our hope on Christ, might live for the praise of *his glory*.

13In him you also, when you had heard the word of truth, the *gospel of your salvation*, and had believed in him, were marked with the *seal* of the promised Holy Spirit; **14**this is the pledge of our inheritance toward *redemption* as God's own people, to the praise of his glory.

---

holy Special, set apart.
destined Implemented a plan of action.
adoption Making people who aren't related to be closely related.
grace Favor, empowerment.
the Beloved Christ.
forgiveness of our trespasses God holds none of our offenses against us.
inheritance A beautiful future gift intended to delight and overwhelm.
his glory God's overwhelming goodness, beauty, power and strength.
gospel of your salvation By his life, death and resurrection Christ brought the kingdom of God in full measure.
seal A sign that we really, truly belong.
redemption Pulling people back from sin and despair.

- Before the foundation of the world, God thought of each of us and decided that we were a good idea—and so created us (verse 4)!

- God gives us blessings "according to his [good] pleasure" (verses 5, 9) because "that's what gave him delight ... just as he wanted it."[1]

- Other:_____

2. Which of these spiritual blessings is most impactful for you?

- God has chosen each of us and thinks about us, including how we can be transformed into a person who is deeply good and pleasing (verses 4, 11).

- God regards each of us as an adopted child, not as strangers or guests who are barely known (verse 5). We are part of the family of God.

- God gives us "glorious grace" (favor and empowerment) "in the Beloved" (verse 6).

- God lavishes forgiveness on us, and deliverance from the sins that have hounded us (verses 7-8).

- God reveals to us "the mystery of his will" ("the secret of his purpose"[2]) with wisdom and insight (verse 8).

- All of this is done "in him" (Christ—verses 3, 4, 6, 7, 9, 10, 11, 13) and through him (verse 5) so that we can have "union with God" here and now.

- Other:_____

3. We're a part of the larger story of God's purpose for the whole cosmos—to build a beloved community to live in God's powerful, personal presence and grace. Heaven and earth will be joined together so that God will dwell with humans in a life without tears (Revelation 21:1-4).

God isn't waiting for us to earn this purpose or build it. God takes the initiative, extends the invitation and empowers us to be a part of the divine plan.

What feelings does this truth elicit in you?

- Wonder at being part of something so enormous
- Gladness that life is not random
- Gladness that the cosmos is not random
- Curiousity about what such a future dwelling place will be like
- Eagerness to experience such beloved community
- Other:_____

4. What does this passage tell you about what God is like? (God's plans, his pleasure, his approach toward humanity)

Reflect on the invitation. Perhaps God is offering you an invitation in this passage to enlarge your understanding about something. What might that be? Read the passage again and then sit quietly for a few minutes, pondering these questions:

- What word, phrase or idea stands out to you?
- Why do you think that is?

Reflect a little further. You may wish to read the passage again. Then consider:

- How does this passage connect with your life?
- Is there something God might be inviting you to think about, or even dream about? What possibilities might God be offering you?
- How does this passage make you feel?

Be open to the quiet and don't feel pressured to come up with an answer.

Respond (*ORATIO*)

Take a few minutes to tell God how you responded to whatever idea that stood out to you in this passage. You may wish to thank God for this invitation and a future of possibilities.

You may ask God questions (the answers to which may come to you later). You may wish to write your prayer down. Sometimes that helps keep our mind from wandering.

Rest (*CONTEMPLATIO*)

Think of "every spiritual blessing" as filling the air around you. Breathe in this rich air and consider what it would be like to live and move in such an atmosphere.

Or consider: How did God (or God's actions) seem to you in this passage?

Trying It On (*INCARNATIO*)

Later today or tomorrow, reflect on whatever task lies before you. Remember that you have been chosen, shaped and empowered by God. How does that task seem different to you in that light?

7

One in Whom Christ Dwells

Ephesians 2:13-22

RELAX AND REFOCUS (*SILENCIO*)

Center yourself by breathing slowly in and out. Relax your neck and take time to let your muscles relax.

Optional—Consider this question: If you were to say that someone "lives on in you" (a parent, grandparent or mentor who has passed away), what would you mean by that?

READ (*LECTIO*)

Read the passage to yourself silently. Then read the notes below it about the key words and phrases. Consider how these details help your understanding of the passage. Then read the passage aloud slowly. Take time to let the words "fall on your ear."

REFLECT (*MEDITATIO*)

Questions and cues to help you reflect on the passage.

  1. *The beloved community: Two groups joined together.* Underline all the phrases in this passage that refer to two groups of people becoming one.

Ephesians 2:13–22

¹³But now in Christ Jesus you who once were far away have been brought near by the blood of Christ.

¹⁴For he himself is our *peace*, who has made the *two groups one* and has destroyed the barrier, the dividing wall of hostility, ¹⁵by setting aside in his flesh the law with its commands and regulations. His purpose was to create in himself one new humanity out of the two, thus making peace, ¹⁶and in one body to reconcile both of them to God through the cross, by which he put to death their hostility. ¹⁷He came and preached peace to you who were far away and peace to those who were near. ¹⁸For through him we both have access to the Father by one Spirit.

¹⁹Consequently, you are no longer foreigners and strangers, but fellow citizens with God's people and also members of his household, ²⁰built on the foundation of the apostles and prophets, with Christ Jesus himself as the chief cornerstone. ²¹*In him* the whole building is joined together and rises to become a holy *temple* in the Lord. ²²And in him you too are being built together to become a dwelling in which God lives by his Spirit.

---

peace Resting in God's goodness[1]—the word *peace* occurs four times in this passage (verses 14, 15 and 17).
two groups one Jews and Gentiles became one group in Christ, united by the Spirit in the church.
In him In Christ; other phrases that communicate our union with Christ: "in Christ Jesus," "in himself," "through him," "with Christ Jesus," "in him," "in him."
temple A place where God dwells.

What are some attributes of a family that you long to find in God?

- belonging
- finding your "tribe"
- having a safety net and knowing you won't fall through the cracks
- having family members you want to be like and spend time with
- Other:_____

2. *Historical and cultural background: A temple is where God dwells (verses 21-22, see also 1 Corinthians 6:19).*[2] N. T. Wright emphasizes that the Jewish temple was "the place where heaven and earth meet." Heaven and earth are not "separated by a great gulf. Instead, they overlap and interlock . . . so that God makes his presence known, seen and heard within the sphere of earth."[3] So every moment is a sacred one as heaven and earth meet within us. We are walking temples. When a server waits on us in a restaurant, when a friend calls, when someone receives our email—they are encountering a walking temple. This is who and what we are and what we were intended to be. Together as a body of Christ we form a temple: a place where God dwells.

How do you respond to this idea that you are a walking temple?

- honored

- skeptical

- overwhelmed

- Other:_____

3. What kind of God would want to live within and among humans? What does that say about God?

4. *Scriptural connections: God's family.* Christ's followers are "fellow citizens" of the kingdom of God (verse 19) and members of God's household—the "family of believers," the children of God (Galatians 6:10; 1 Peter 2:17; 1 John 3:1). Building this family is Trinitarian work.

- God the Father (verses 16, 19, 22)

- Christ (verses 13, 14, 17, 18, 20, 21, 22)

- the Holy Spirit (verses 18, 22)

Reflect on the invitation. Read the passage again and then sit quietly for a few minutes, pondering these questions:

- What word or phrase stands out to you?

- Why do you think that is?

   Reflect a little further. You may wish to read the passage again. Then consider:

- How does this passage connect with your life?

- Is there some idea, feeling or intention you need to embrace from it? If so, what is it?

- What might God be inviting you to be, know, understand, feel or even do?

Be open to the quiet and don't feel pressured to come up with an answer.

Respond (*ORATIO*)

What do you wish to say to Christ about belonging to God's family or about being "in Christ"?

Rest (*CONTEMPLATIO*)

"Contemplation" comes from the Latin word *contemplationem*. *Com* means "with"; *templum* is the Latin word for "temple." Take a few minutes to just *be* with God, to enjoy being one in whom God dwells. Open yourself to simply abiding with or resting in God.

Trying It On (*INCARNATIO*)

Consider how you interact with those in God's beloved community. Do they seem different to you in the light of this passage? How might you promote the idea that the followers of Jesus are part of the beloved community?

The "Sanctified" Imagination

Half of the exercises in this book focus on narratives and invite you to enter into them by imagining the setting and the actions of the passage and then watching the events unfold. You observe them as if you were a fly on the wall, watching it all happen. The questions and cues help you wonder, If I had been present, what would I have seen, heard, tasted, touched or smelled?

This approach works well today because we're used to watching movies. We read the passage and picture it as a movie. If a scene in one of these meditations involves Jesus, you are asked imagine the expression on Jesus' face based on the words he says. We may even identify ourselves with the person Jesus is speaking to. When that happens, let Jesus look you in the eyes and speak to you as he did the person in the passage. This isn't about inserting unwarranted feelings or expressions for Jesus, because such meditation relies heavily on the Scripture for clues, which is why studying words and parallel passages is important. It is still Word-centered and guided by the Spirit. We imagine his facial expression to be congruent with his character (that as God, he is love and speaks truth in love). Thus we find ourselves addressed directly by Jesus.

You may protest that you have a weak imagination, but in truth everyone uses their imagination powerfully and frequently. How? When you worry! Yes, the imagination can be used for evil, but it can be "sanctified" to help us with our faith. When the Jews celebrated Passover, they re-enacted the original setting and action (wearing traveling clothes, eating the foods from the original Passover). When Jesus presented parables, he was asking listeners to imagine certain scenes he made up.

Meditation then renews our imagination as we picture Christ and other biblical people in real events of history. Such retraining of the imagination takes practice, but it is slowly reconfigured by the mind of Christ (1 Corinthians 2:16). As our imaginations are fueled with "stories, images and hopes drawn from God's history with the people of God, [they] can become a penetrating force."[1]

8

An Identity
Completely Changed

Luke 8:26-39

RELAX AND REFOCUS (*SILENCIO*)

Inhale and exhale a few times. Let go of distractions. Quiet your thoughts
and open yourself to God.

Optional—Consider this question to focus your thoughts on today's
passage: What nicknames have you been given in the past? Were they
complimentary and encouraging? Or demeaning and discouraging?

READ (*LECTIO*)

Read the passage to yourself. Then read the notes below it about the key
words and phrases. Consider how these details affect your understanding
of the story. Then read the passage aloud slowly. Take time to let the
words "fall on your ear."

REFLECT (*MEDITATIO*)

Questions and cues to help you enter into the story.

1. In Mark's version of this story we find some more details about this
   man. "No one was strong enough to subdue him. Night and day
   among the tombs and in the hills he would cry out and cut himself

Luke 8:26-39

26 They sailed to the region of the **Gerasenes**, which is across the lake from Galilee. **27** When Jesus stepped ashore, he was met by a **demon-possessed man** from the town. For a long time this man had not worn clothes or lived in a house, but had lived in the **tombs**. **28** When he saw Jesus, he cried out and fell at his feet, shouting at the top of his voice, "What do you want with me, Jesus, Son of the Most High God? I beg you, don't torture me!" **29** For Jesus had commanded the impure spirit to come out of the man. Many times it had seized him, and though he was chained hand and foot and kept under guard, he had broken his chains and had been driven by the demon into solitary places.

30 Jesus asked him, "What is your name?"

"**Legion**," he replied, because many demons had gone into him. **31** And they begged Jesus repeatedly not to order them to go into **the Abyss**.

32 A large herd of pigs was feeding there on the hillside. The demons begged Jesus to let them go into the pigs, and he gave them permission. **33** When the demons came out of the man, they went into the pigs, and the herd rushed down the steep bank into the lake and was drowned. **34** When those tending the pigs saw what had happened, they ran off and reported this in the town and countryside, **35** and the people went out to see what had happened. When they came to Jesus, they found the man from whom the demons had gone out, sitting at Jesus' feet, dressed and in his right mind; and they were afraid. **36** Those who had seen it told the people how

---

Gerasenes This Gentile region southeast of the Sea of Galilee included ten self-governing cities (collectively called Decapolis) that had been settled centuries earlier by Greek traders and immigrants.

demon-possessed man Demons are beings with intelligence and personality who work destruction on behalf of Satan.

tombs These were usually hewn out of caves on the shore. Living in a graveyard (as well as being a Gentile and demon-possessed) made this man ceremonially unclean. Teachers like Jesus normally had no dealings with ceremonially unclean people.

Legion The largest unit in the Roman army, having from three to six thousand soldiers.

the Abyss The bottomless pit where Satan will be banished for a time (Revelation 20:3).

the demon-possessed man had been cured. **37** Then all the people of the region of the Gerasenes asked Jesus to leave them, because they were overcome with fear. So ***he got into the boat*** and left.

38 The man from whom the demons had gone out begged to go with him, but Jesus sent him away, saying, **39** "Return home and tell how much God has done for you." So the man went away and told all over town how much Jesus had done for him.

---

he got into the boat Was Jesus the only one who had ever gotten out of the boat? Had the man terrified Jesus' disciples so badly that they stayed in the boat?

---

with stones" (Mark 5:4-5). Based on what you see in the text, how did the townspeople seem to regard the demon-possessed man? What did they probably feel about him? Consider these clues in the text.

- Maybe the man had been tortured, since he asked Jesus not to torture him (Luke 8:28).
- The townspeople had chained him hand and foot and hired a guard (Luke 8:29).
- No one had been strong enough to subdue him (Mark 5:4).

2. In the first century, names indicated something true about the person. How did the name "Legion" reflect this man's identity?

The man formerly called Legion was found "sitting at Jesus' feet" (verse 35), which was a way of saying that he had become a disciple of Jesus. Jesus must have spent some time teaching and interacting with the man. As a result, Jesus urged him to "tell how much God has done for him" (verse 39). The man seems to have done a good job, because when Jesus arrived later in this region, people already knew who he was (Mark 6:54).

3. What identities—originating from circumstances, life issues or past behaviors—would you like to let go? Write these in the first column. What new identities might Christ want to give you? If you did the two previous meditations, you may want to think about identity in terms of being blessed with every spiritual blessing, being chosen and adopted, and being part of God's family.

Former identity	New identity
Example: I am often negative and defensive	*I can think about how I might bless others*

4. *Fly on the wall cue: Picture the stampede.* The stampede of the pigs that received the demons and plunged into the sea is important. Their loss was tragic (especially to their owner). The stampede pictures the flight of the man's demons from him. It would have created a dust cloud that would have been seen for miles, and served as testimony that the demons had truly left the man. This proof of freedom and cleansing from the demons was important for the townspeople to see, so that they would accept the man back into society and not try to chain him up once again. In a sense, the pigs partnered with Jesus in creating a picture of the man's new freedom.

If you wish, picture this dust cloud. How must it have looked to the man? Consider how it looked to the townspeople, who would have naturally suspected that a demon or two still lived in the man.

5. *Fly on the wall cue: Picture the change in the man.* Close your eyes and imagine the man raving and screaming, perhaps holding up those strong arms that had broken the chains. Then imagine him sitting at Jesus' feet, dressed and in his right mind. Hear the loud noise first and then the serene quiet.

Reflect on the invitation. Read the passage aloud again. Picture what the scene would look like. Hear the words clearly.

- As you picture the events of the passage, what moment, action or phrase is most real to you? What does this cause you to think and feel?
- Why might that moment, word or phrase have stood out to you?

Reflect a little further. Read the passage again and picture what the scene might look like as if you were watching a movie. Hear the words clearly in your mind.

- How does this passage connect with your life?
- Is there some idea, feeling or intention you need to embrace from it? If so, what?
- What might God be inviting you to be, know, understand, feel or even do?

Be open to the quiet and don't feel pressured to come up with an answer.

RESPOND (*ORATIO*)

Tell Jesus how you respond to his ability to transform this man's life. Talk with Jesus about any renewal or clarity of identity that you need today.

REST (*CONTEMPLATIO*)

Sit in the quiet, noting that the demon-possessed man was settled and quiet, and possibly quite excited about his new life. The screaming and tormenting thoughts were only a memory.

How did Jesus (or Jesus' actions) seem to you in this passage? What does this tell you about what God is like?

Spend a few minutes soaking in the thoughts that have come to you. This may take the form of worship or simply resting in God's presence.

TRYING IT ON (*INCARNATIO*)

Take another look at the third question above. Write down any ideas that come to you. You might ask God for a few more ideas.

Life in the Spirit

Romans 8:1-11, 14

RELAX AND REFOCUS (*SILENCIO*)

Center yourself by breathing in and out. Take time to let your muscles relax.

Optional—If you need to focus, you may wish to use this prayer as you begin:

> Let us release the cares of our day,
> and open our eyes to the wonder of God.
> With an attitude of empathy to people of another time,
> let us open our hearts and minds to God.
> Let us prepare to experience God's Word to us through the
> presence of the Holy Spirit.

READ (*LECTIO*)

Read the passage to yourself silently. Then read the notes below it about the key words and phrases. Consider how these details help your understanding of the passage. Then read the passage aloud slowly. Take time to let the words "fall on your ear."

Romans 8:1–11, 14

¹Therefore, there is now no condemnation for those who are **in Christ Jesus**, ²because through Christ Jesus the **law of the Spirit** who gives life has set you free from the **law of sin and death**. ³For what **the law was powerless** to do because it was weakened by the flesh, God did by sending his own Son in the likeness of sinful flesh to be a sin offering. And so he condemned sin in the flesh, ⁴in order that the **righteous requirement of the law might be fully met** in us, who do not **live according to the flesh** but according to the Spirit.

⁵Those who live according to the flesh have their minds set on what the flesh desires; but those who **live in accordance with the Spirit** have their minds set on what the Spirit desires. ⁶The mind governed by the flesh is death, but the mind governed by the Spirit is life and peace. ⁷The mind governed by the flesh is hostile to God; it does not submit to God's law, nor can it do so. ⁸Those who are in the realm of the flesh cannot please God.

⁹You, however, are not in the realm of the flesh but are in the realm of the Spirit, if indeed the Spirit of God lives in you. And if anyone does not have the Spirit of Christ, they do not belong to Christ. ¹⁰But if Christ is in you, then even though your body is subject to death because of sin, the Spirit gives life because of righteousness. ¹¹And if the Spirit of him who

---

in Christ Jesus Union with Christ—this includes multiple dimensions such as following Christ and abiding in Christ.

law of the Spirit . . . law of sin and death "Law" here refers to the principles, ideas or even facts of something. So we might say, "The Spirit who gives life sets us free from the facts of sin and death through Christ Jesus."

the law was powerless The Old Testament law was a good and wonderful thing (see Psalm 119), but it did not have the power (the Spirit) to help us live by it.

righteous requirement of the law might be fully met "Those who obey the law of love are in fact fulfilling the moral commands of the *Torah*."[1] Through the Spirit we move toward becoming the good and loving people the Old Testament law described (Deuteronomy 6:5; Leviticus 19:18).

live according to the flesh To act according to what people naturally do, which can be good or evil. The apostle Paul had fleshly confidence in his qualifications as a righteous Jew (Philippians 3:5-6).[2]

live in accordance with the Spirit To live a life empowered by the Spirit.

> raised Jesus from the dead is living in you, he who raised Christ from the dead
> **will also give life to your mortal bodies** because of his Spirit who lives in you.
> **¹⁴**For those who are led by the Spirit of God are the **children of God**.
>
> ---
>
> **will also give life to your mortal bodies** The abundant life that Christ can give to us
> on earth (John 6:33) as well as life after we die.
> **children of God** Just as physical children resemble their parents, children of God
> resemble his Son Jesus.

REFLECT (*MEDITATIO*)

Questions and cues to help you reflect on the passage.

1. *Living according to the Spirit.* What great differences would we see in people living according to the Spirit rather than the normal, natural way people live (by the flesh)? If you're not sure, you might think about the ideas contained in passages like 1 Corinthians 13 or Matthew 5–7.

Natural life (led by the flesh)	Supernatural life (led by the Spirit)
example: Tolerating people	Loving people

2. *A "mind that is governed by the flesh" (verse 6).* In his book *Renovation of the Heart,* Dallas Willard describes the "mind of the flesh" as making our own desires paramount and investing only in our natural selves.[3]

How does making "my desires paramount" and "invest[ing] only in one's natural self" create a life of misery?

3. *The Spirit living in people.* The Spirit works in the hearts of believers:

   - to generate faith itself by the preaching of the gospel;
   - to generate the kind of life where our minds are focused on what the Spirit desires, resulting in life and peace; and

- to work powerfully on the other side of death to give new bodily life.[4]

4. *Inviting the Spirit in.* How can we pay attention to the Spirit, give our minds to the Spirit and let our lives be animated by the Spirit?

5. *Fly on the wall cue: Imagine what Paul's inner connection to God was like.* Paul, our older brother in the faith, appeals to us in this passage, saying, "Human beings in their natural state, faced with God's law, are about as much use as a gas lamp plugged into the electric supply."[5] As you imagine powerful events in Paul's life (healings, getting up again after being stoned, encouraging his children in the faith), consider that his "gas lamp" must have been plugged directly into a natural gas well.

Reflect on the invitation. Perhaps God is offering you an invitation in this passage to enlarge your understanding about something. What might that be? Read the passage again and then sit quietly for a few minutes, pondering these questions:

- What word or phrase stands out to you?
- Why do you think that is?

Reflect a little further. You may wish to read the passage again. Then consider:

- How does this passage connect with your life?
- Is there some idea, feeling or intention you need to embrace from it? If so, what is it?
- What might God be inviting you to be, know, understand, feel or even do?

Be open to the quiet and don't feel pressured to come up with an answer.

Respond (*ORATIO*)

Take a few minutes to respond to God about this in prayer. Tell God what you think about this passage. Tell the Spirit what you think and feel about his living within you.

Rest (*CONTEMPLATIO*)

Soak in what has stood out to you in this passage. You might want to sing the well-known hymn "Spirit of the Living God, Fall Fresh on Me," or another appropriate song.

Trying It On (*INCARNATIO*)

Make a short list of simple practices that help your mind focus on the things the Spirit desires. Try one out and consider how doing this re-adjusts your attitude.

Blessed to Be a Blessing

Genesis 12:1-5; 21:1-7

RELAX AND REFOCUS (*SILENCIO*)

Inhale and exhale a few times. Let go of distractions. Quiet your thoughts and open yourself to God.

Optional—If you need help focusing, ponder this question: When have you enjoyed helping or supporting someone in some way?

READ (*LECTIO*)

Read the passage to yourself. Then read the notes below it about the key words and phrases. Consider how these details affect your understanding of the story. Then read the passage aloud slowly. Take time to let the words "fall on your ear."

REFLECT (*MEDITATIO*)

Questions and cues to help you enter into the story.

1. *Cultural background: The importance of children.* The Hebrews regarded the presence of children in the family as a mark of divine favor and greatly to be desired. The birth of a male child was especially a cause for rejoicing. To Hebrew women, childlessness was the greatest of misfortunes (Genesis 15:2; 30:1, 23; 1 Samuel 1:11, 20; Psalms 127:3; 128:3; Luke 1:7, 28).[1]

Genesis 12:1–5; 21:1–7

¹The LORD had said to Abram, "Go from your country, your people and your father's household to the land I will show you.

²"I will make you into a great nation,
    and I will ***bless*** you;
I will make your name great,
    and you will be a blessing.
³I will bless those who bless you,
    and whoever curses you I will curse;
and ***all peoples on earth***
    will be blessed through you."

⁴So Abram went, as the LORD had told him; and Lot went with him. ***Abram was seventy-five years old*** when he set out from Harran. ⁵He took his wife Sarai, his nephew Lot, ***all the possessions they had accumulated and the people they had acquired in Harran***, and they set out for the land of Canaan, and they arrived there.

¹Now the LORD was gracious to Sarah as he had said, and the LORD did for Sarah what he had promised. ²Sarah became pregnant and bore a son to Abraham in his old age, at the very time God had promised him. ³Abraham gave the name Isaac to the son Sarah bore him. ⁴When his son Isaac was

---

bless The Hebrew words *barak* (Strong's 1288) and *arar* (Strong's 779)—"to bless" and "to curse"—are found throughout the Old Testament. When blessings and cursings were spoken formally they carried a special significance, and had the power to bring about their own fulfillment.

all peoples on earth will be blessed through you This prophecy was repeated three more times (Genesis 18:18; 22:18; 26:4). Ultimately, all people benefit from the coming of Christ through Abraham's descendants (compare Acts 3:25; Galatians 3:8).

Abram was seventy-five years old . . . was a hundred years old Twenty-five years elapsed between the promise and its fulfillment.

all the possessions they had accumulated and the people they had acquired in Harran Abram and Sarai appear to have been very rich (see also Genesis 13:2; 14:23).

eight days old, Abraham circumcised him, as God commanded him. ⁵Abraham ***was a hundred years old*** when his son Isaac was born to him.

⁶Sarah said, "God has brought me laughter, and everyone who hears about this will laugh with me." ⁷And she added, "Who would have said to Abraham that Sarah would nurse children? Yet I have borne him a son in his old age."

How do you think Abraham and Sarah felt before the promise was given? They were rich in livestock, silver and gold, yet they were childless (Genesis 13:2). How might their feelings have changed after Isaac was born?

2. *Scriptural connections: Partnering with God.* Giving Abraham and Sarah a child was an opportunity for them to be partners in God's grand vision of building "a kingdom of priests and a holy nation" from which Jesus would come. The result of this would be the beloved community God had envisioned before the foundation of the world (Exodus 19:6; Ephesians 1:4). The words of the Abrahamic promise indicated that the child and the nation would benefit all the people of the earth and be a light to the Gentiles, just as Jesus was the light of the world (Genesis 12:3; Isaiah 42:6; 49:6; John 9:5). Paul echoes this idea by saying that God comforts us, and we pass on this comfort to others (2 Corinthians 1:3-4).

How might this view of God blessing us to be a benefit to others enhance our identity or sense of partnership with God?

- We notice better how God blesses us.

- We feel honored to join God in blessing others.

- Because we understand that God is working through us to help others, we're more likely to ask God for guidance about how to be a blessing to someone. *do I ask God*

- Other:_____

3. What are the qualities of people who automatically use their blessings to help others? For example, when they get a raise they might think, *Whom can I bless with this surplus?* instead of just, *What can I buy for myself now?*

- lightness of spirit

- the ability to see others' needs

- willingness to serve others

- a sense of adventurous partnership with God

- Other:_____

4. *Fly on the wall cue: Picture Abraham's compound.* Abraham, Sarah and their servants were seminomadic people who lived in tents, but their tents were probably rather grand and stayed in place for years at a time. They were surrounded by their many flocks, herds and possessions.

Picture Abraham and Sarah holding their newborn son and thinking about God's promise all those years ago: "All peoples on earth will be blessed through you." This referred to people they would never meet, from all eras of history—including you. Their twenty-five years of patient waiting and the challenges of rearing a son in their old age would result in exponential blessing for the whole world.

Reflect on the invitation. Read the passage again and picture what the scene might look like as if you were watching a movie. Hear the words clearly in your mind.

- As you watch the action unfold, what do you see?

- What moment in the story, or what word or phrase stands out to you? What does this make you think and feel?

- Why do you think that is? What significance might this have for you?

Reflect a little further.

- How does this passage connect with your life?

- Is there some idea, feeling or intention you need to embrace from it? If so, what is it?

- What might God be inviting you to be, know, understand, feel or even do?

Be open to the quiet and don't feel pressured to come up with an answer.

RESPOND (*ORATIO*)

Take a few minutes to respond to God about this in prayer. What do you most want to say to God about being blessed to be a blessing—or any other idea that came to you? What feelings or thoughts rise up within you?

REST (*CONTEMPLATIO*)

Soak in what has stood out to you in this passage and consider: How did God (or God's character and actions) seem to you in this passage? What does this tell you about what God is like?

Consider that when God made the promise to Abram—"all peoples on earth will be blessed through you"—God was including you in this blessing.

TRYING IT ON (*INCARNATIO*)

Ask God to show you how you might partner with him in using what you are and what you have to be a blessing to others. Thank God for this partnership.

Scripture Study and Meditation Work Together

To study Scripture is to dissect the biblical text. We may research the meaning of words, compare the text with parallel passages, or investigate the biblical and historical context. This guide does a lot of that work for you.

To meditate on Scripture is different from study. Instead of dissecting it, we savor the text and hold it in our minds, allowing time for God to speak to us. Study of Scripture involves analytical reading for information, while meditation on Scripture is an attentive style of reading for formation of our soul.

Study and meditation complement each other. Both are important to individual Christians and the church as a whole. If we study but neglect meditation, we can know many facts about the Bible but be experientially ignorant both of God's presence and of how God is speaking to us.

It's almost as if we're attempting to master the text—when in fact God is the master of the text. We delight in learning something new, but not so much in knowing God. If we meditate alone, however, we are more likely to misinterpret the straightforward ideas of Scripture, and as a result we can incorrectly sense what God is saying. What is learned in the study of Scripture keeps us from reading fanciful interpretations into Scripture. It also opens up a rich world of context (which enhances meditation) that might otherwise be missed because of time and cultural distance. To approach Scripture meditatively is to submit to the Spirit's searching gaze. Through meditation, what we see cognitively in study speaks to our entire beings—calling us into wholeness.

11

Relying on the Kingdom of God

Matthew 6:10, 25-34

RELAX AND REFOCUS (*SILENCIO*)

Center yourself by breathing in and out. Relax your neck and take time to let your muscles relax.

Optional—To settle in a little more, think about this idea: *I have everything I need.* What color does that idea bring to mind? Why?

READ (*LECTIO*)

Read the passage to yourself silently. Then read the notes below it about the key words and phrases. Consider how these details help your understanding of the passage. Then read the passage aloud slowly. Take time to let the words "fall on your ear."

REFLECT (*MEDITATIO*)

Questions and cues to help you reflect on the passage.

1. Consider these paraphrases of "seek first his kingdom" (verse 33). Which versions do you find most engaging?

   • Strive to be a part of what God is actually doing on earth now and the goodness with which God is doing it.[1]

Matthew 6:10, 25-34

¹⁰Your **kingdom** come,
your will be done,
     on earth as it is in heaven.

²⁵"Therefore I tell you, do not worry about your life, what you will eat or drink; or about your body, what you will wear. Is not life more than food, and the body more than clothes? ²⁶Look at the birds of the air; they do not sow or reap or store away in barns, and yet your heavenly Father feeds them. Are you not much more valuable than they? ²⁷Can any one of you by worrying add a single hour to your life?

²⁸"And why do you worry about clothes? See how the flowers of the field grow. They do not labor or spin. ²⁹Yet I tell you that not even **Solomon in all his splendor** was dressed like one of these. ³⁰If that is how God clothes the grass of the field, which is here today and tomorrow is thrown into the fire, will he not much more clothe you—you of little faith? ³¹So do not worry, saying, 'What shall we eat?' or 'What shall we drink?' or 'What shall we wear?' ³²For the pagans run after all these things, and your heavenly Father knows that you need them. ³³But seek first his kingdom and his **righteousness**, and all these things will be given to you as well. ³⁴Therefore do not worry about tomorrow, for tomorrow will worry about itself. Each day has enough trouble of its own."

---

kingdom "The kingdom of God is the range of [God's] effective will: that is, it is the domain where what he prefers is actually what happens."[2] God's kingdom is in power wherever God's will is done.

Solomon in all his splendor This refers to the vast wealth and glamour of Solomon's court. To get the meaning we might substitute the name of a very rich person or a model.

righteousness The Greek word, *dikaiosynē* (Strong's 1343), means deep, attractive inner goodness. "The best translation of *dikaiosynē* would be a paraphrase: something like 'what that is about a person that makes him or her really right or good.' For short, we might say 'true inner goodness.'"[3]

- "Place top priority on identifying and involving [our]selves in what God is doing and in the kind of righteousness [*dikaiosynē*] he has. All else needed is provided."[4]

- "Steep your life in God-reality, God-initiative, God-provisions. Don't worry about missing out. You'll find all your everyday human concerns will be met. Give your entire attention to what God is doing right now, and don't get worked up about what may or may not happen tomorrow. God will help you deal with whatever hard things come up when the time comes" (*The Message*).

2. What do you think God is actually doing right now in the world? In people you know? In groups you are part of? In you?

3. Imagine that Jesus is speaking the words in this passage directly to you. Remember that he knows what matters most to you. How might he complete this line (from verse 25): *Is not life more than _____?* Mark as many as you find appropriate.

   - the food you crave
   - owning the latest styles of clothing
   - advancing in your career
   - having a classy car, house or apartment
   - being a perfect parent, spouse or coworker
   - having a body that others admire
   - achieving more than anyone else in your family has achieved
   - crossing off every item on today's to-do list
   - other people's good opinion of you
   - Other:_____

4. *Fly on the wall cue: Picture Jesus teaching.* This passage is part of the Sermon on the Mount (Matthew 5–7), so you might imagine Jesus

saying these things as he sits or stands on a hillside. Envision people laughing as Jesus talks about someone who worries very hard because he thinks that will help him live a few days longer, or someone who is so enchanted by wild flowers that she doesn't notice her favorite film star walking by. What might Jesus' facial expressions and tone of voice have been as he talked about how everything is provided in the kingdom of God? Base this on what you know of him (he was friendly to children, he could speak passionately).

Reflect on the invitation. Perhaps God is offering you an invitation in this passage to enlarge your understanding about something. What might that be? Read the passage again and then sit quietly for a few minutes, pondering these questions:

- What word or phrase stands out to you?
- If you pictured Jesus saying these words, what do you notice?
- Why do you think that is?

Reflect a little further. You may wish to read the passage again. Then consider:

- How does this passage connect with your life?
- Is there some idea, feeling or intention you need to embrace from it? If so, what?
- What might God be inviting you to be, know, understand, feel or even do?

Be open to the quiet and don't feel pressured to come up with an answer.

RESPOND (*ORATIO*)

Take a few minutes to respond to God about this. What do you most want to say to God about this experience in Scripture? About the idea that everything we need is provided to us in the kingdom of God?

You may wish to ask God questions (the answers to which may come to you later). You may wish to write out your prayer. Sometimes that helps to keep our mind from wandering.

Rest (*CONTEMPLATIO*)

Soak in this idea: *In the kingdom, you have everything you need.* What would your life be like if you trusted that this was true?

Spend a few more minutes noticing the thoughts that have come to you.

Trying It On (*INCARNATIO*)

Try to notice actions and attitudes around you that reflect people doing what God wants done. Thank God for these glimpses.

Relying on the Kingdom, Illustrated

Daniel 6

RELAX AND REFOCUS (*SILENCIO*)

Inhale and exhale a few times. Let go of distractions. Quiet your thoughts and open yourself to God.

Optional—Consider this question: When, if ever, have you been in a situation you never would have chosen? How did you respond? Was it easy to depend on God or not?

READ (*LECTIO*)

Read the passage to yourself. Then read the notes below it about the key words and phrases. Consider how these details affect your understanding of the story. Then read the passage aloud slowly. Take time to let the words "fall on your ear."

REFLECT (*MEDITATIO*)

Questions and cues to help you enter into the story.

1. How might Daniel have coped with being a Jew in Babylon? What might have been some of his thoughts? Consider some of the facts of Daniel's background and character.

Daniel 6:3-7, 10-11, 13-14, 16, 19-23, 26-27

³Now *Daniel* so distinguished himself among the administrators and the *satraps* by his exceptional qualities that the king planned to set him over the whole kingdom. ⁴At this, the administrators and the satraps tried to find grounds for charges against Daniel in his conduct of government affairs, but they were unable to do so. They could find no corruption in him, because he was trustworthy and neither corrupt nor negligent. ⁵Finally these men said, "We will never find any basis for charges against this man Daniel unless it has something to do with the law of his God."

⁶So these administrators and satraps went as a group to the king and said: "May King Darius live forever! ⁷The royal administrators, prefects, satraps, advisers and governors have all agreed that the king should issue an edict and enforce the decree that anyone who prays to any god or human being during the next thirty days, except to you, Your Majesty, shall be thrown into the lions' den."

¹⁰Now when Daniel learned that the decree had been published, he went home to his upstairs room where the windows opened toward Jerusalem. Three times a day he got down on his knees and prayed, giving thanks to his God, just as he had done before. ¹¹Then these men went as a group and found Daniel praying and asking God for help.

¹³Then they said to the king, "Daniel, who is one of the exiles from Judah, pays no attention to you, Your Majesty, or to the decree you put in writing. He still prays three times a day." ¹⁴When the king heard this, he was greatly distressed; he was determined to rescue Daniel and made every effort until sundown to save him.

¹⁶So the king gave the order, and they brought Daniel and threw him into the lions' den. The king said to Daniel, "May your God, whom you serve continually, rescue you!"

Daniel A Jewish teenager who had been taken captive and had served first the Babylonians and now Darius, king of the Persians. He would have been about eighty years old by this time.
satraps Governors or "kingdom-protectors."[1]

76 MEETING GOD IN SCRIPTURE

19At the first light of dawn, the king got up and hurried to the lions' den. **20**When he came near the den, he called to Daniel in an anguished voice, "Daniel, servant of the living God, has your God, whom you serve continually, been able to rescue you from the lions?"

21Daniel answered, "May the king live forever! **22**My God sent his angel, and he shut the mouths of the lions. They have not hurt me, because I was found innocent in his sight. Nor have I ever done any wrong before you, Your Majesty."

23The king was overjoyed and gave orders to lift Daniel out of the den. And when Daniel was lifted from the den, no wound was found on him, because he had trusted in his God.

26"I issue a decree that in every part of my kingdom people must fear and reverence the God of Daniel.
"For he is the living God
and he endures forever;
his kingdom will not be destroyed,
his dominion will never end.
27He rescues and he saves;
he performs signs and wonders
in the heavens and on the earth."

his kingdom will not be destroyed Darius recognized that Daniel's God was a powerful being with a "kingdom"—a place where whatever God wanted done was done (even by lions).

- When the powerful nation of Babylon invaded the southern tribe of Judah, King Nebuchadnezzar destroyed the temple and took all its treasures. He and his army took captives from Judah back to Babylon (about five hundred miles away) and made them slaves. Daniel was educated and put to work in the government. If Daniel was about sixteen years old when he was taken captive (605 BCE) he would have been at least eighty-two in this account (since the Persians captured Babylon in about 539 BCE).

- No mention is ever made of Daniel being bitter. Instead he seemed to grow close to and even fond of his captor, Nebuchadnezzar.

- The text notes that Daniel was "trustworthy and was neither corrupt nor negligent" (verse 4).

2. Darius seems to have fallen prey to flattery through the proposal that his subjects pray to him and no one else. When have you suffered the consequences of someone in authority over you making an unwise decision? How did you feel? What did you do?

3. Which part of Darius's description of the kingdom of God is most meaningful for you today (verses 26-27)?

- God is a living God, not a "force" or barely in existence.

- God perseveres and never gives up.

- The kingdom of God is indestructible (endures forever).

- God rescues people and brings wholeness.

- God does miraculous things on earth and in the cosmos.

4. Daniel exhibited exemplary character. He never sought honor or personal gain. He was a trustworthy and incorruptible government official. He became friends with kings who could easily have been his enemies. The key to his character was his relationship with God, cultivated in the many spiritual disciplines he practiced:

- fasting and healthy eating (1:8, 12; 9:3; 10:3)

- prayer (2:18, 20-23; 6:10; 9:3, 20)

- confession (9:4, 20)

- service (6:4, 5)

- study of Scripture (9:2, 23; 10:12)

- frugality (5:17)

- worship (2:20-23)

How do these disciplines contribute to a person's character?

5. *Fly on the wall cue: Picture Daniel in the pit.* Edward J. Young writes
   that "in all probability there was an opening at the top through which
   Daniel had been lowered into the den, and through which the king
   later spoke with Daniel, and also an opening at the side through
   which the lions were fed. It was probably such a side entrance which
   was closed by the stone and seal; the entrance at the top was evidently
   too high for any man to escape through it."[2]

6. *Scriptural connections: Jesus and his kingdom.* The kingdom of God
   existed in Old Testament times (Psalm 145:13; Daniel 2:44; 7:14,
   27), but Jesus brought the kingdom of God to earth in a new way,
   saying, "The kingdom of God is in your midst" (Luke 17:21; see also
   Matthew 12:28; Luke 10:9-10). We will experience the kingdom in
   an even fuller way at the end of this age (Revelation 11:15).

7. *Scriptural connections: Kingdom of God timeline.* The kingdom was in
   existence even in Old Testament times. The table below shows how
   the revelation of the kingdom of God unfolds.

Reflect on the invitation. Read the passage aloud again. Picture what
the scene might look like as if you were watching a movie. Hear the
words clearly in your mind.

- As you watch the action unfold, what do you see?

- What moment or idea in the story stands out to you? Imagine what
  Daniel may have thought or felt. Does this resonate with you?

- Why do you think that is? What significance might this have
  for you?

  Reflect a little further.

- How does this passage connect with your life?

- Is there some idea, feeling or intention you need to embrace from it?
  If so, what?

Before Jesus Came	Daniel, who lived in pagan Babylon after Israel's temple was destroyed, spoke of an everlasting kingdom and understood that it would never be destroyed (2:44; 4:3; 6:26). The psalmist spoke of the glorious splendor of God's everlasting kingdom (Psalm 145:11-13).
During Jesus' Life	Jesus brought the kingdom of God to earth in a fuller way so that the kingdom was *near* to his hearers. Jesus said the kingdom was "on your doorstep" (Luke 10:9, 11, *The Message*), and "in your midst" (Luke 17:21). Jesus' teaching was centered on the kingdom of God (see, for example, Mark 1:15; 4:11-30; 10:14-15). Jesus displayed the presence of the kingdom with miraculous works of power and authority.
Jesus' Post-resurrection Preaching	His topic was the kingdom of God (Acts 1:3).
The Early Church Through the Present	The apostles taught the kingdom of God (Acts 8:12; 14:22; 19:8; 28:23, 31) and manifested it through miraculous works (Acts 3:1-10; 5:12-16; 9:34; 14:9). Paul spoke of himself and his companions as "coworkers in the kingdom of God" (Colossians 4:11; see also Romans 14:17; 1 Corinthians 4:20).
At Jesus' Return and Afterward	The kingdom of God will be realized in a fuller way (Luke 22:16, 18) with God reigning as King in fullness (Revelation 22:4-5).

- What might God be inviting you to be, know, understand, feel or even do?

Be open to the quiet and don't feel pressured to come up with an answer.

RESPOND (*ORATIO*)

Take a few minutes to respond to God about this in prayer. What do you most want to say to God about this experience in Scripture?

REST (*CONTEMPLATIO*)

Soak in what has stood out to you in this passage and consider: How did God (or God's actions) seem to you in this passage? What does this tell you about what God is like?

Spend a few minutes noticing the thoughts that have come to you. This may take the form of worship or simply resting in God's presence.

Trying It On (*INCARNATIO*)

Consider kneeling and thanking God (verse 10) for sustaining you in situations that have felt awkward.

Openness to the Spirit

We like to exert control over what we see and hear—such as watching television without commercials, for instance. We also try to manage or control the Bible by seeking out verses that seem to prove what we already believe to be true or hope is true. We come to the Bible looking for a solution to a particular problem and read it through that lens. Our Scripture study and meditation should be free from such maneuvering. Instead, we should seek to surrender control to the Holy Spirit. We should let the text stand on its own and wait to see how the Spirit may address us through it.

*Such vulnerability to the Spirit requires that we "welcome with meekness the implanted word that has the power to save your souls" (James 1:21 NRSV). We ought to come to the Word ready to hear whatever the Spirit might have to say to us. We should be careful not to make anything up based on what we **want** to hear. What comes to us may not be new or exceptional. It may be something we already know, but we need to embrace it at a deeper level. Or perhaps it is exactly what we need to hear today—right now—because of life circumstances.*

A. W. Tozer describes this phenomenon:

> [The Bible] is not only a book which was once spoken, but a book which is now speaking. . . . If you would follow on to know the Lord, come at once to the open Bible expecting it to speak to you. Do not come with the notion that it is a thing which you can push around at your convenience.[1]

We "push around" Scripture by interpreting it within preconceived ideas of what it means, or what it means for us today. Trying to cover as much material as we can in a hurried manner generally blocks vulnerability or meekness (and how they help us sense what God is saying). The goal of interaction with God in the Word is not to finish a chapter or book, but to meet God.

Dr. Robert Mulholland calls this experience of God speaking to us through Scripture "dynamic inspiration." He says the phrase "All Scripture is inspired by God" (2 Timothy 3:16-17 NRSV) is translated in various ways because Paul intended several layers of meaning. The inspiration of Scripture is "dynamic" because, in addition to the writer of the book being inspired, the Spirit also inspires us as we read it.[2]

We will find it easier to be open to the Spirit's inspiration if we keep a "holding pattern" over the words or phrases that stand out to us. This openness to the Spirit allows God to address a problem we thought we had solved, a relationship we thought had healed or a conclusion we've already made but that needs to be rethought. The meditation experience may help us "re-see" a situation so that we understand the heart of the other person and have a mercy we didn't have before. We come away with the eyes of our hearts enlightened (Ephesians 1:18).

13

The Hidden Yet Powerful
Kingdom of God

Matthew 13:24-32, 36-40

RELAX AND REFOCUS (*SILENCIO*)

Center yourself by breathing in and out. Relax your neck and take time
to let your muscles relax.

Optional—Ponder this question: What are some things that are
hidden, yet powerful? For example, electricity itself isn't usually seen, but
we see its powerful effects. What else?

READ (*LECTIO*)

Read the passage to yourself silently. Then read the notes below it about
the key words and phrases. Consider how these details help your understanding of the passage. Then read the passage aloud slowly. Take time
to let the words "fall on your ear."

REFLECT (*MEDITATIO*)

Questions and cues to help you enter into the story.

1. *Characters focus: Farmer, enemy and slaves (verses 24-30).* Do you see
   yourself in any of the characters in the parable of the weeds or its
   explanation? Are you

Matthew 13:24-32, 36-40

24Jesus told them another parable: "The ***kingdom of heaven*** is like a man who sowed good seed in his field. **25**But while everyone was sleeping, his enemy came and sowed weeds among the wheat, and went away. **26**When the wheat sprouted and formed heads, then the weeds also appeared.

27"The owner's servants came to him and said, 'Sir, didn't you sow good seed in your field? Where then did the weeds come from?'

28"'An enemy did this,' he replied.

"The servants asked him, 'Do you want us to go and pull them up?'

29"'No,' he answered, 'because while you are pulling the weeds, you may uproot the wheat with them. **30**Let both grow together until the harvest. At that time I will tell the harvesters: First collect the weeds and tie them in bundles to be burned; then gather the wheat and bring it into my barn.'"

31He told them another parable: "The kingdom of heaven is like a ***mustard seed***, which a man took and planted in his field. **32**Though it is the smallest of all seeds, yet when it grows, it is the largest of garden plants and becomes a tree, so that the birds come and perch in its branches."

36Then he left the crowd and went into the house. His disciples came to him and said, "Explain to us the parable of the weeds in the field."

37He answered, "The one who sowed the good seed is the ***Son of Man***. **38**The field is the world, and the good seed stands for the people of the kingdom. The weeds are the people of the evil one, **39**and the enemy who sows them is the devil. The harvest is the end of the age, and the harvesters are angels.

40"As the weeds are pulled up and burned in the fire, so it will be at the end of the age."

---

kingdom of heaven Matthew calls the kingdom of God the "kingdom of heaven," perhaps because Jews avoid saying God's name, or perhaps because Matthew wanted to emphasize the kingdom's nearness. The Jews thought of heaven as beginning on the surface of the earth—the air around us—and extending upward.
mustard seed The small round seeds of mustard plants are usually 1 or 2 millimeters in diameter. They can be yellowish white or black.
Son of Man Jesus' way of referring to himself.

- the diligent owner who plants wheat seed in his field?

- the enemy who sneaks in at night to scatter weeds in the field?

- the bewildered servants who ask how this bad thing could have happened?

- the solution-oriented servants who want to go gather up the weeds?

- the harvesters (angels) who collect both the wheat and the weeds?

- the owner who waits for what he thinks is the best moment to act—delaying the removal of the weeds in order to protect the precious wheat harvest?

- the people of the kingdom who live side by side with people of the evil one?

Why do you identify with that character? If you identified with any of the servants, how difficult would it be for you to trust the owner?

(When you read the passage again later in this section, the Spirit may prompt you to identify with a different character.)

2. Does anything about Jesus' explanation of the parable of the weeds surprise or startle you?

- Power and hiddenness don't seem to go together. Powerful people are usually visible, not hidden. But in these parables the powerful kingdom of God is always hidden in some way.

- In the weeds parable, the separation between wheat and weeds is delayed, although the power of the growth of the wheat crop does not seem to be affected.

- In the mustard seed parable, an item so small that it could easily be overlooked or thrown away grows into the biggest thing in the garden, which provides for others exactly what they need.

3. God's method of delay and hiddenness contradict today's preferences for prominence, flashiness and self-promotion. In the kingdom of God, values often seem upside down. Reading about the power of the kingdom is encouraging. How do you respond to the idea that the kingdom is often hidden and delayed?

- frustrated
- puzzled
- impressed
- Other:_____

Why do you think you respond that way?

4. Jesus used imagery of everyday objects and activities in his teaching. As I wrote elsewhere, he seemed to "pick up whatever was within arm's reach and show how it resembled the kingdom of God. He took whatever was at hand—a vine, tree, seed, plow, yoke, coin—and did this. One time when the disciples argued, he took a child in his arms and declared, 'Unless you change and become like children ...' (Matthew 18:1-6).... Consider that Jesus was such an insightful teacher that if he were sitting next to you, he could pick up any [household] item and explain how the kingdom of God was just like that item."[1]

Look at what is within arm's reach of you right now. Is there any way it could be compared to the kingdom of God?

- the richness of taste and deep satisfaction of a good cup of coffee
- water, a fundamental necessity of life
- an afghan that keeps you warm
- a reading lamp that makes it possible for you to read even when it's dark
- Other:_____

Reflect on the invitation. Read the passage again and then sit quietly for a few minutes, pondering these questions:

- What word or phrase stands out to you?

- Why do you think that is?

- Perhaps God is offering you an invitation in this passage to enlarge your understanding about God and his kingdom. What might that be?

Reflect a little further. You may wish to read the passage again. Then consider:

- How does this passage connect with your life?

- Is there some idea, feeling or intention you need to embrace from it? If so, what is it?

- What might God be inviting you to be, know, understand, feel or even do?

Be open to the quiet and don't feel pressured to come up with an answer.

RESPOND (*ORATIO*)

Take a few minutes to respond to what you have heard from God. What do you most wish to say to God about this experience in Scripture?

REST (*CONTEMPLATIO*)

Soak in what has stood out to you in this passage and consider: How did God (or God's actions) seem to you in this passage?

Spend a few minutes noticing the thoughts that have come to you. This may take the form of worship or simply resting in God's presence.

TRYING IT ON (*INCARNATIO*)

Look for circumstances or persons who seem hidden in their influence yet are still powerful. If nothing comes to you, ask God to help you see them.

14

The Hidden Yet Powerful Kingdom of God, Illustrated

2 Kings 6:15-23

RELAX AND REFOCUS (*SILENCIO*)

Slowly inhale and exhale a few times. Let go of distractions. Quiet your thoughts and open yourself to God.

Optional—If you need help focusing, think of times when fire has seemed beautiful or majestic to you.

READ (*LECTIO*)

Read the passage to yourself. Then read the notes below it about the key words and phrases. Consider how these details affect your understanding of the story. Then read the passage aloud slowly. Take time to let the words "fall on your ear."

REFLECT (*MEDITATIO*)

Questions and cues to help you enter into the story.

1. *Character background: Elisha.*

   • Miracle worker: Elisha's miracles often met simple human needs— for example, finding a lost axe head that provided someone's

2 Kings 6:15-23

¹⁵When the servant of **the man of God** got up and went out early the next morning, **an army with horses and chariots had surrounded the city**. "Oh no, my lord! What shall we do?" the servant asked.

¹⁶"Don't be afraid," the prophet answered. "Those who are with us are more than those who are with them."

¹⁷And Elisha prayed, "Open his eyes, Lord, so that he may see." Then the Lord opened the servant's eyes, and he looked and saw the hills full of **horses and chariots of fire** all around Elisha.

¹⁸As the enemy came down toward him, Elisha prayed to the Lord, "Strike this army with blindness." So he struck them with blindness, as Elisha had asked.

¹⁹Elisha told them, "This is not the road and this is not the city. Follow me, and I will lead you to the man you are looking for." And he led them to Samaria.

²⁰After they entered the city, Elisha said, "Lord, open the eyes of these men so they can see." Then the Lord opened their eyes and they looked, and there they were, inside Samaria.

²¹When the king of Israel saw them, he asked Elisha, "Shall I kill them, **my father**? Shall I kill them?"

²²"Do not kill them," he answered. "Would you kill those you have captured with your own sword or bow? **Set food and water before them** so

---

the man of God Elisha, a prophet to the northern tribes of Israel.

an army with horses and chariots had surrounded the city The Aramean army, which Israel was fighting. The king of Aram wanted to seize Elisha because he faithfully (and miraculously) reported what the king said even in his bedroom to the king of Israel, giving Israel an advantage in battle. This entire army was sent to capture Elisha.

horses and chariots of fire This resembles the armies of heaven in Revelation, led by a white horse and a rider with eyes like a flame of fire (Revelation 19:11, 14; see also Psalm 68:17), or the supernatural chariots that Ezekiel saw (Ezekiel 1:13-21).

my father The king of Israel at this time had a great respect for Elisha.

Set food and water before them Elisha wants to feed Israel's enemy and send them to safety.

that they may eat and drink and then go back to their master." **23**So he prepared a great feast for them, and after they had finished eating and drinking, he sent them away, and they returned to their master. So the **bands from Aram stopped raiding** Israel's territory.

bands from Aram stopped raiding Marauding parties were no longer permitted by the Aramean king to enter Israel.

livelihood and pulling the poison out of a mess of pottage so that it was edible by his followers (2 Kings 6:4-7; 4:38-41).

- Highly esteemed: The king of Aram sent an entire army to capture one man, Elisha.

- Comfortable with the invisible: Elisha already knew the chariots of fire were present. He spoke about them to reassure his servant, who was afraid (verse 16).

- Secure: Elisha was unafraid. He understood that he lived in "a kingdom that cannot be shaken" (Hebrews 12:28).

- Not a showoff: Elisha wanted the servant's eyes to be opened because this met the servant's need, not to show off. Elisha illustrated the apostle Paul's words about the unseen: "Therefore we do not lose heart. Though outwardly we are wasting away, yet inwardly we are being renewed day by day. For our light and momentary troubles are achieving for us an eternal glory that far outweighs them all. So we fix our eyes not on what is seen, but on what is unseen, since what is seen is temporary, but what is unseen is eternal" (2 Corinthians 4:16-18).

- Possessed eyes of faith: Eyes of faith see the reality of divine presence and protection. The horses and chariots were symbols of divine power, and their fiery nature signified the divine presence. These eyes of faith seem to equip Elisha to operate in the power of the kingdom.

What is most intriguing to you about Elisha?

2. *Scriptural connections: Fire.*

- God's presence and power were often signified by fire. For instance, think about the blazing firepot in God's covenant with Abraham (Genesis 15:17), the burning bush (Exodus 3:2-4), the pillar of fire that led the Israelites in the wilderness (Exodus 13:21), the fire on Mt. Sinai (Exodus 19:18) and the flame on Manoah's altar (Judges 13:20). Yahweh was "the God who answers by fire" (1 Kings 18:24, 38).

- Fire was involved in offerings and sacrifices. In Leviticus 9:24, the sacrificial fire "came out from the presence of the LORD." Fire from Yahweh signified the acceptance of certain special and separate sacrifices (Judges 6:21; 1 Kings 18:38; 1 Chronicles 21:26). The altar-fire was to be kept continually burning (Leviticus 6:12, 13); offering "strange fire" was punished by "fire from the presence of the LORD" (Leviticus 10:1, 2). Fire also came from heaven at the consecration of Solomon's temple (2 Chronicles 7:1).[1]

- "The manifestation in atmospheric fire became almost a routine event in Israel's history, so much so that God came to be known as a consuming fire (Deut. 4:24; Heb. 12:29)—a fire that is also love."[2]

Why does fire make an appropriate substance to represent God's presence?

3. *Fly on the wall: Picture chariots and the kingdom of God.* The horses and chariots of fire resemble the armies of heaven in Revelation, led by a white horse and a rider with eyes like a flame of fire (Revelation 19:11, 14; see also Psalm 68:17), or the supernatural chariots and horses that Ezekiel saw: bright creatures like torches with fire moving

back and forth among them and lightning flashing out of them (Ezekiel 1:13-21).

The chariots in the heavenly realm were ready to do whatever God wanted. They secured a kingdom space, which Elisha easily accessed.[3]

What do you think was the servant's response to seeing the chariots of fire? How do you think he may have felt?

Reflect on the invitation. Read the passage aloud again. Picture what the scene would look like. Hear the words clearly.

- As you watch the action unfold, what do you see?
- What do you think Elisha, his servant or Israel's king may have been feeling in this story? Does that resonate with you?
- Why do you think that is? What significance might this have for you?

Reflect a little further.

- How does this passage connect with your life?
- Is there some idea, feeling or intention you need to embrace from it? If so, what is it?
- What might God be inviting you to be, know, understand, feel or even do?

Be open to the quiet and don't feel pressured to come up with an answer.

RESPOND (*ORATIO*)

Take a few minutes to respond to God about this. What do you most want to say to God about this experience in Scripture?

REST (*CONTEMPLATIO*)

Soak in what has stood out to you in this passage and consider: How did God (or God's actions) seem to you in this passage? What does this tell you about what God is like?

Spend a few minutes noticing the thoughts that have come to you. This may take the form of worship or simply resting in God's presence.

TRYING IT ON (*INCARNATIO*)

Pick one of these phrases to call to mind throughout your day:

- "I live in the unshakeable kingdom of God" (see Hebrews 12:28 *The Message*).

- "Those who are with us are more than those who are with them" (2 Kings 6:16).

The Good and Peaceable Kingdom of God

Isaiah 11:1-9

RELAX AND REFOCUS (*SILENCIO*)

Center yourself by breathing in and out. Relax your neck and take time to let your muscles relax.

Optional—If you need help setting in and focusing, ask God to bring to mind places in the world that need the peace of the kingdom life (nations, neighborhoods, cultural groups or relationships of people you know).

READ (*LECTIO*)

Read the passage to yourself silently. Then read the notes below it about the key words and phrases. Consider how these details help your understanding of the passage. Then read the passage aloud slowly. Take time to let the words "fall on your ear."

REFLECT (*MEDITATIO*)

Questions and cues to help you reflect on the passage.

1. Verses 6-9 paint a picture of the kingdom of God in the future, when there will be no sorrow, death or pain (Revelation 21:4). The entire passage is often referred to as "The Peaceable Kingdom."[1]

Isaiah 11:1-9

1A shoot will come up from the **stump of Jesse**;
   from his roots **a Branch will bear fruit**.
2The Spirit of the LORD will rest on him—
   the Spirit of wisdom and of understanding,
   the Spirit of counsel and of might,
   the Spirit of the knowledge and fear of the LORD—
3and he will delight in the fear of the LORD.

He will **not judge by what he sees with his eyes**,
   or decide by what he hears with his ears;
4but with righteousness he will judge the needy,
   with justice he will give decisions for the poor of the earth.
He will **strike the earth with the rod of his mouth**;
   with the breath of his lips he will slay the wicked.
5Righteousness will be his belt
   and faithfulness the sash around his waist.

6The **wolf will live with the lamb**,
   the leopard will lie down with the goat,
the calf and the lion and the yearling together;
   and a little child will lead them.

---

stump of Jesse The stump was all that remained of the tree of the house and descendants of David (whose father was Jesse). The last king in that line was tortured and taken captive to Babylon, where he died (Jeremiah 52:11).
a Branch will bear fruit Out of the dead stump, a tender shoot grows, which becomes a branch that bears miraculous fruit. This Branch is the Messiah.
not judge by what he sees with his eyes This Messiah won't judge by appearances or hearsay but by what is right and just, empowered by the Spirit. This further hints at the Messiah being more than a human.
strike the earth with the rod of his mouth This Messiah's words will command the attention of people; his breath will overthrow the wicked. (Proverbs 25:15—"A gentle tongue can break a bone.")
wolf will live with the lamb This and the following verses describe animals that are natural enemies being at peace with each other.

> **7**The cow will feed with the bear,
>   their young will lie down together,
>   and the lion will ***eat straw*** like the ox.
> **8*The infant will play near the cobra's den*,**
>   and the young child will put its hand into the viper's nest.
> **9**They will neither harm nor destroy
>   on all my holy mountain,
> **for the earth will be filled with the knowledge of the LORD**
>   as the waters cover the sea.

---

eat straw The lion will no longer kill its prey for food but will eat straw instead.
the infant will play near the cobra's den This kingdom will be so peaceable that deadly snakes won't harm children.
for the earth will be filled with the knowledge of the LORD All nations (not just Israel) will know God.

"Each animal is coupled with one that would naturally be its prey, a situation only possible under the 'Prince of Peace' (65:25; Ezek. 34:25; Hos. 2:18) when a return to the relationships of animals and man experienced in the Garden of Eden is realized."[2]

If Isaiah lived in our time and culture, what natural enemies might he have included in the peaceable kingdom? Try naming a few.

- dueling political parties

- rival nations

- rival sports teams

- Other:_____

Now consider how odd it would be for these two groups/persons to live together in peace, as they do in this passage.

2. In verses 1-5,

- What is the most attractive thing about the Messiah?

- What is the most astonishing thing about the Messiah?

In verses 6-9,

- What is the most attractive thing about the messianic kingdom?
- What is the most astonishing thing about the messianic kingdom?

Reflect on the invitation. Perhaps God is offering you an invitation in this passage to enlarge your understanding about something. What might that be? Read the passage again and then sit quietly for a few minutes, pondering these questions:

- What word or phrase stands out to you?
- Why do you think that is?

Reflect a little further. You may wish to read the passage again. Then consider:

- How does this passage connect with your life?
- Is there some idea, feeling or intention you need to embrace from it? If so, what is it?
- What might God be inviting you to be, know, understand, feel or even do?

Be open to the quiet and don't feel pressured to come up with an answer.

RESPOND (*ORATIO*)

Take a few minutes to respond to God about this. What do you most want to say to God about what has stood out to you in this passage?

REST (*CONTEMPLATIO*)

Soak in the deep goodness and peace of this passage. How do you find your body responding to that? Are you smiling? Exhaling?

Spend a few minutes noticing the thoughts that have come to you. This may take the form of worship or simply resting in God's presence.

TRYING IT ON (*INCARNATIO*)

Picture any troublesome circumstances in the world today as they would be in the peaceable kingdom.

Experiment with moving through your day seeking first God's kingdom and righteousness. You might want to use these words: "Give your entire attention to what God is doing right now, and don't get worked up about what may or may not happen tomorrow" (Matthew 6:34 *The Message*).

Am I Hearing God or Making Things Up?

When insights or ideas come to you as you meditate on Scripture, you may wonder, Is God bringing this to my mind? Or is this my subconscious playing the same old tapes and thinking patterns in my head? Or is the enemy trying to sabotage me?

As you meditate on Scripture more, you'll become more skilled at recognizing God's voice and learning to differentiate it from your own. For example, "The voice of the subconscious argues with you, tries to convince you; but the inner voice of God does not argue, does not try to convince you. It just speaks. It has the feel of the voice of God within it."[1] Generally speaking, what we hear from God will sound nothing like our own self-talk, particularly if you are plagued with worry or negative thinking.

Making something up is a subtle version of controlling the meditation yourself rather than letting God give you insight. You might ask yourself: Am I writing the script or receiving it? Am I able to be surprised by what comes to me? What God most often communicates through Scripture meditation is not some new revelation, but a practical insight, an idea that is freeing for you today or something that is a culmination of what you know, but couldn't quite grasp.

If you're unsure whether the insight that has come to you is from God, you might run it by someone wiser than you. This is a matter of learning to hear God's voice. You are building communication skills with the heavenly Father.

Consider that Scripture meditation is the most reliable place to hear God. Dallas Willard put it this way: "More of God's speaking to me has come in conjunction with study and teaching of the Bible than with anything else."[2]

Abiding in Christ

John 15:1-11

RELAX AND REFOCUS (*SILENCIO*)

Center yourself by breathing in and out. Relax your neck and take time to let your muscles relax.

Optional—If you wish, consider this quotation from Andrew Murray to focus your thoughts on today's passage:

> Who would learn to abide in Jesus, take time each day, ere you read, and while you read, and after you read, to put yourself into living contact with the living Jesus, to yield yourself distinctly and consciously to His blessed influence, so you will give Him the opportunity of taking hold of you, of drawing you up and keeping you safe in His almighty life.[1]

As you quiet yourself, rest your hands in your lap, placing your hands palms down as a symbol of turning over any concerns you have. If a nagging thought arises, turn your hands palms up as a "symbol of your desire to receive from the Lord."[2] If you become distracted at any time during meditation, repeat the exercise.

READ (*LECTIO*)

Read the passage to yourself silently. Then read the notes below it about the key words and phrases. Consider how these details help your

John 15:1-11 (NRSV)

¹I am the **true vine**, and my Father is the vinegrower. ²He removes every branch in me that bears no fruit. Every branch that bears fruit he **prunes** to make it bear more fruit. ³You have already been cleansed by the word that I have spoken to you. ⁴**Abide** in me as I abide in you. Just as the branch cannot bear fruit by itself unless it abides in the vine, neither can you unless you abide in me.

⁵I am the vine, you are the branches. Those who abide in me and I in them bear much fruit, because apart from me you can do nothing. ⁶Whoever does not abide in me is thrown away like a branch and withers; such branches are gathered, thrown into the fire, and **burned**. ⁷If you abide in me, and my words abide in you, **ask for whatever you wish**, and it will be done for you. ⁸My Father is **glorified** by this, that you bear much fruit and become my disciples.

⁹As the Father has loved me, so I have loved you; abide in my love. ¹⁰If you keep my commandments, you will abide in my love, just as I have kept my Father's commandments and abide in his love. ¹¹I have said these things to you so that my **joy** may be in you, and that your joy may be complete.

true vine Prophets often described Israel as a vine or vineyard, but usually as a useless or degenerate vine that yielded wild or even bad grapes (Isaiah 5:1-7; Ezekiel 15:1-6). Jesus is saying that he is the authentic vine.

prunes This resembles the idea in verse 3 of the disciples being cleansed and freed from distracting ambitions to follow Jesus.

Abide The Greek word is menō (Strong's 3306), which means to remain or abide, to continue, dwell, endure, be present, stay, stay in contact with.

burned Withered branches work well in a bonfire, which is useful, but not as useful as a branch attached to the vine and bearing fruit.

ask for whatever you wish If we are abiding in the vine, our requests have come through the vine, which is Christ.

glorified God is glorified when divine beauty, goodness, power and strength are made obvious to others.

joy A pervasive sense of well-being.[3]

understanding of the passage. Then read the passage aloud slowly. Take time to let the words "fall on your ear."

REFLECT (*MEDITATIO*)

Questions and cues to help you reflect on the passage.

1. *Scriptural connections: Fruit (verses 2, 4, 5, 8).* Some identify *fruit* here as the fruit of the Spirit from Galatians 5:22-23 (love, joy, peace, patience, kindness, goodness, faithfulness, gentleness and self-control) or perhaps virtue in general, while others insist that *fruit* refers to those who respond to evangelistic efforts, which seems to be the meaning in John 4:35-38.

> But something more basic, something that underlies both missionary work and ethical virtues, seems to be intended. The development of the image in vv. 7-17 suggests that bearing fruit refers to the possession of the divine life itself and especially the chief characteristics of that life, knowledge of God (cf. 15:15) and love (15:9-14). Jesus says when they bear much fruit they demonstrate that they are his disciples (15:8), and elsewhere he names love as the evidence that one is a disciple (13:35; 14:21, 23) and is in union with God and with one another (17:21-23). Thus, the image of fruit symbolizes that which is at the heart of both Christian witness and ethics—union with God.[4]

How do you respond to the idea that union (or oneness) with God is not only possible but likely as we abide in Christ? Check as many as apply.

- I've never thought about it before.

- It seems beyond me or my experience.

- I want it!

- I am hungry for oneness with a God—a real sense of *belonging*.

- Other:_____

2. *Scriptural connections: Pruning.* Jesus told his disciples that they were the branches (verse 5) and that branches could expect to be pruned (verse 2). Pruning has been interpreted to mean various things, but the text shows that pruning is something that God does. Pruning is the work of the Spirit to remove hindrances from a person's heart, cleansing their thoughts or even taking away sinful tendencies (1 Thessalonians 5:23-24).

The quotation from Andrew Murray above (in the relax and refocus section) spoke of putting yourself "into living contact with the living Jesus, to yield yourself distinctly and consciously to His blessed influence."[5] This can be experienced in all of life: Christ has prepared for you an "abiding dwelling with Himself, where your whole life and every moment of it might be spent, where the work of your daily life might be done, and where all the while you might be enjoying unbroken communion with Himself."[6]

What does contact with God (or abiding in Christ) look like in your life?

What activities help put you in contact with God?

- being in nature: hiking, walking by a lake or ocean
- holding a baby
- meditating on Scripture
- serving someone in need
- preparing to teach a class
- talking with fellow Christians about faith
- talking about faith with those who are exploring faith
- sitting quietly watching the sun rise or set
- Other:_____

3. Andrew Murray writes that, "The believer can each day be pleasing to God only in that which he does through the power of Christ

dwelling in him. The daily inflowing of the life-sap of the Holy Spirit is his only power to bring forth fruit. He lives alone in Him and is for each moment dependent on Him alone."[7]

- Underline the words or phrases from this quote that have to do with abiding in Christ.

- Circle the words or phrases that have to do with obedience to Christ.

- Put a box around the words or phrases that have to do with the transformation of our character.

4. The abiding life produces joy (verse 11). Why might that be? How might obedience be involved in this?

5. *Fly on the wall cue: Picture the branches.* Dead branches are dry and snap when they are bent. But living branches have juices or sap in them that make them difficult to cut. Because juices are still flowing into them, cutting them takes sharp pruners. Imagine that you are a branch and that the sap of the vine is being imparted to you.

Reflect on the invitation. This passage offers an explicit invitation—or perhaps an instruction, since it's given as an imperative: Abide! How does that strike you? Are there other invitations for you in this passage? If so, what might they be? Read the passage again and then sit quietly for a few minutes, pondering these questions:

- What words or phrases stand out to you?

- Why do you think that is?

Reflect a little further. You may wish to read the passage again. Then consider:

- How does this passage connect with your life?

- Is there some idea, feeling or intention you need to embrace from it? If so, what is it?

- What might God be inviting you to be, know, understand, feel or even do?

Be open to the quiet and don't feel pressured to come up with an answer.

RESPOND (*ORATIO*)

Take a few minutes to respond to God about this. What do you most want to say to God about this meditation in John 15:1-11?

You may wish to ask God questions, especially about what abiding looks like for you. You may wish to write your prayer down. Sometimes that keeps our mind from wandering.

REST (*CONTEMPLATIO*)

Soak in the main idea or phrase that has stood out to you. Consider that the energy needed to live a rich, full life is absorbed from the presence of Christ who abides in you, not by trying to feel or be anything.

Spend a few minutes noticing the thoughts that have come to you. This may take the form of worship or simply resting in God's presence.

TRYING IT ON (*INCARNATIO*)

Take a walk, a hike or even a bike ride and experiment with what it's like to abide in Christ in the middle of an everyday activity.

From Gangster to Giver

Luke 19:1-10

RELAX AND REFOCUS (*SILENCIO*)

Center yourself by breathing in and out. Relax your neck and take time to let your muscles relax.

Optional—If you need to focus, ponder this question: Who is someone you know whom you would be shocked to discover decided to follow Christ?

READ (*LECTIO*)

Read the passage to yourself. Then read the notes below it about the key words and phrases. Consider how these details affect your understanding of the story. Then read the passage aloud slowly. Take time to let the words "fall on your ear."

REFLECT (*MEDITATIO*)

Questions and cues to help you enter into the story.

1. What are some possible reasons that a gangster like Zacchaeus was willing to go to such lengths to see Jesus? He not only put himself at risk to be hurt by a crowd of people who no doubt hated him, but also shamed himself by perching in a tree.

Luke 19:1-10

¹Jesus entered Jericho and was passing through. ²A man was there by the name of Zacchaeus; he was a ***chief tax collector*** and was wealthy. ³He wanted to see who Jesus was, but because he was short he could not see over the crowd. ⁴So he ran ahead and ***climbed a sycamore-fig tree*** to see him, since Jesus was coming that way.

⁵When Jesus reached the spot, he looked up and said to him, "Zacchaeus, come down immediately. I must stay at your house today." ⁶So he came down at once and welcomed him gladly.

⁷All the people saw this and began to mutter, "He has gone to be the guest of a sinner."

⁸But Zacchaeus stood up and said to the Lord, "Look, Lord! Here and now I give half of my possessions to the poor, and if I have cheated anybody out of anything, I will pay back four times the amount."

⁹Jesus said to him, "Today ***salvation*** has come to this house, because this man, too, is a son of Abraham. ¹⁰For the Son of Man came to seek and to save the lost."

---

chief tax collector Chief tax collectors were hated and considered unclean. They skimmed money off the income of other tax collectors, who in turn skimmed money off Jewish citizens. Lying to them was condoned.[1]

climbed a sycamore-fig tree Zacchaeus needed to climb the tree not just because he was short, but also because it wouldn't have been safe for such a hated man to walk unprotected in a crowd. A man like Zacchaeus would not typically have shamed himself by climbing a tree, but perhaps he thought the leafy sycamore tree would shield him from view.

salvation The Greek word, *sōtēria* (Strong's 4991), means rescue or safety (physically or morally), to be delivered, or health.

- He had heard about Jesus from other tax collectors.

- He had heard that one of Jesus' disciples had been a tax collector (Matthew).

- He had heard Jesus teach before, perhaps in Jerusalem.

- His wife had heard Jesus teach and told Zacchaeus about him.
- Other:_____

2. If you had been in the crowd, what would you have expected a rabbi to say to Zacchaeus?

- You're a very bad person. Return these people's money now!
- You must change your ways. Come and study with me.
- Why are you betraying Israel and working for Rome?
- Other:_____

How might you have responded to Jesus interacting with Zacchaeus and insisting on staying at his house?

3. Jesus had intended only to "pass through" Jericho (verse 1). In other words, Jesus wasn't planning on staying there overnight. He seems to have changed his mind when he saw Zacchaeus in the tree.

If you had been one of the disciples traveling with Jesus and had been invited to stay at Zacchaeus's house with Jesus, this might have appalled or disgusted you. Even though Jesus normally befriended those who were poor and oppressed (widows and beggars), it would have been unusual for Jesus to spend time with a wealthy oppressor. Would you have agreed to stay at Zacchaeus's home or would you have refused? Why?

4. *Fly on the wall cue: Picture the setting.* Look over the story and picture the large crowd following Jesus and the huge overhanging sycamore tree. Imagine a well-dressed, wealthy man sitting on one of the branches.

5. *Fly on the wall cue: Picture Jesus' actions and facial expressions.* We don't know how Jesus knew Zacchaeus's name. Perhaps he overheard the crowd around him laughing about seeing Zacchaeus in the tree. Jesus

stopped deliberately, called Zacchaeus by name, and invited himself to Zacchaeus's house (the last one being something your mother told you never to do). Jesus' words and facial expression elicited a glad welcome from Zacchaeus. What might Jesus' face have looked like when he called out to him?

Reflect on the invitation. Read the passage aloud again. Picture what the scene might have looked like as if you were watching a movie. Hear the words clearly in your mind.

- As you watch the action unfold, what do you see?
- What moment or idea in the story stands out to you and resonates with you?
- Why do you think that is? What significance might this have for you?
  Reflect a little further.
- How does this passage connect with your life?
- Is there some idea, feeling or intention you need to embrace from it? If so, what is it?
- What might God be inviting you to be, know, understand, feel or even do?

Be open to the quiet and don't feel pressured to come up with an answer.

RESPOND (*ORATIO*)

Take a few minutes to respond to God about this. What do you most want to say to God about this experience in Scripture?

REST (*CONTEMPLATIO*)

Soak in what has stood out to you in this passage and consider: How did Jesus (or Jesus' actions) seem to you in this passage? What does this tell you about what God is like?

Spend a few minutes noticing the thoughts that have come to you. This may take the form of worship or simply resting in God's presence.

TRYING IT ON (*INCARNATIO*)

Look for a "Zacchaeus" in your world (or maybe it's you)—someone who hasn't treated others well. Ask God what you need to know about this person. Even if God doesn't lead you to do anything in regard to this person, consider how God might view him or her.

When Your Mind Wanders

If you live an active, hurried lifestyle, you may find this contemplative style of Scripture reading to be challenging. As you're settling in, your mind may come up with a list of things to do. You may find yourself falling asleep. Here are some ideas to bring peace and patience to your wandering, distracted mind.

__Preventing distractions.__ As Chester P. Michael and Marie C. Norrisey tell us, it helps to "choose the time of the day when we are most alert, least distracted, least tired, most well-rested, and without outside pressure."[1] For some people that's when they first wake up; for others, it might be midmorning or before sleeping. It also helps to meditate on Scripture in a place where everything you need is convenient (Bible, journal, colored pens).

If you're easily distracted, take advantage of the optional suggestions in "Relax and Refocus." When you read the passage, do so aloud and slowly to keep you mind focused on the words. Writing prayers down also keeps you focused. Most people find that their cell phone needs to be turned off and put out of reach.

__Dismissing distractions.__ Trying not to be distracted usually makes things worse. It works better to replace your distracted thought with a phrase from Scripture such as "Be still, and know that I am God" (Psalm 46:10) or "The Lord my God is with me" (Zephaniah 3:17).

You might also try rereading the "Questions and cues to help you" section and then closing your eyes again. Sometimes it helps to keep a piece of paper nearby where you can write down things you need to do later. Then set aside the paper in a deliberate way, saying, "This is for later."

Gently include your distracting thoughts in your prayer. Now and then you may have a sense that the distraction needs to be addressed (maybe you thought about praying for a friend). In that case, include the distraction in your prayer. At other times the distraction is a worry that you need to bring to God and see how the passage in front of you addresses it. You may even need to meditate on a different passage that more closely addresses that need.

Most importantly, don't scold yourself when your mind wanders. This is normal. Gently set the distraction aside without annoyance. Ask God to help you.

Letting Go of the Old Self

Colossians 3:1-11

RELAX AND REFOCUS (*SILENCIO*)

Inhale and exhale a few times. Let go of distractions. Quiet your thoughts and open yourself to God.

Optional—If you need help focusing, consider this question: What about your "old self" has God been nudging you to relinquish?

READ (*LECTIO*)

Read the passage to yourself silently. Then read the notes below it about the key words and phrases. Consider how these details help your understanding of the passage. Then read the passage aloud slowly. Take time to let the words "fall on your ear."

REFLECT (*MEDITATIO*)

Questions and cues to help you reflect on the passage.

1. *Glowing phrases.*

   "Set your hearts on things above" (verse 1). To set your heart on things above is to focus your attention on Christ's command to love God and love others, so that life with Christ becomes like a radio station playing within you.

Colossians 3:1-11

¹Since, then, you have been raised with Christ, set your **hearts** on things above, where Christ is, seated at the right hand of God. ²Set your minds on things above, not on earthly things. ³For you **died**, and your life is now hidden with Christ in God. ⁴When Christ, who is your life, appears, then you also will appear with him in glory.

⁵Put to death, therefore, whatever belongs to your earthly nature: sexual immorality, impurity, lust, evil desires and greed, which is idolatry. ⁶Because of these, the wrath of God is coming. ⁷You used to walk in these ways, in the life you once lived. ⁸But now you must also rid yourselves of all such things as these: anger, rage, malice, slander, and filthy language from your lips. ⁹Do not lie to each other, since you have taken off your old self with its practices ¹⁰and have put on the new self, which is being renewed in knowledge in the image of its Creator. ¹¹Here there is no Gentile or Jew, circumcised or uncircumcised, barbarian, **Scythian**, slave or free, but Christ is all, and is in all.

hearts The central part of a person, the same as the will or the spirit, evidenced by the way a person responds to a situation. "The response is our unique contribution to reality. It is ours, it is *us*, as nothing else is."[1]
died Dying to self, that is, to our self-absorbed way of being.
Scythian The rudest of barbarians, they had "filthy habits and never washed in water; they drank the blood of the first enemy killed in battle and made napkins of the scalps and drinking bowls of the skulls of the slain."[2]

What is life like for the person who focuses their attention and puts their energy into loving God and loving others? How is life different for such a person? What do they stop worrying about?

"Your life is now hidden with Christ in God" (verse 3). Life with Christ is "hidden" in the sense that the evidence of the indwelling Christ-life is not in externals only (words, actions that religious people say and do), but is an inner life with God, a oneness that comes from abiding in Christ (John 15:4) and from the Spirit dwelling in that person (Romans 8:11).

What feeling does this idea of being "hidden in Christ" evoke within you?

- feeling safe
- feeling overlooked, because I'm hidden
- feeling like I belong
- feeling like there's hope that I can change because the Spirit dwells in me
- Other:_____

"Christ, who is your life" (verse 4). Christ himself is our new, implanted, divine life. To be saved is to be "rescued from the dominion of darkness and brought us into the kingdom of the Son he loves" (Colossians 1:13). "Those who are saved are to have a *different order of life* from that of the unsaved. . . . God's seminal redemptive act toward us is the communication of a new kind of life, as the seed—one of our Lord's most favored symbols—carries a new life into the enfolding soil. . . . That life will be poised to become a life of the same quality as Christ's, because it indeed is Christ's. He really does live on in us."[3]

Does this awaken any sense of longing in you? If so, what for? If not, why not?

"Old self" and "new self" (verses 9, 10). As the old self is transformed into a new self, we are being "renewed in knowledge in the image of our Creator" (verses 9, 10). This rich phrase has been paraphrased in these ways:

- We are being "progressively renovated to the point of fully sharing in the mind of the creator."[4]
- "Our knowledge of reality is being conformed to the viewpoint of our Creator."[5]
- We begin "to see things as they really are in God's view."[6]

Underline any idea or phrase in these paraphrases that particularly resonates with you. Why is that idea or phrase significant to you?

"Christ is all, and is in all" (verse 11). All humans are God's creatures and redemption in Christ is available to all. Life with God isn't more predisposed to some groups than others, such as Jews rather than Gentiles. Paul's inclusion of the brutal Scythians underlines his point that everyone is included in God's salvation.

Is there a group of people (a certain profession, social status or ethnicity) that you are particularly glad is included in Christ's invitation to this new life?

2. *Fly on the wall: Paul's "Sermon on the Mount."* This teaching resembled many ideas from Jesus' sermon in Matthew 5–7 (not setting the heart on food and drink, but seeking first God's righteousness; laying aside lust and anger; the total goodness of Christ as the perfect example). Did Paul perhaps envision this as his version of the Sermon on the Mount? Did he go to bed the night before he wrote this going over the Sermon on the Mount and thinking, *This is crucial for people to know?*

Reflect on the invitation. Perhaps God is offering you an invitation in this passage to enlarge your understanding about something. What might that be? Read the passage again and then sit quietly for a few minutes, pondering these questions:

- What word or phrase stands out to you?

- Why do you think that is?

Reflect a little further. You may wish to read the passage again. Then consider:

- How does this passage connect with your life?

- Is there some idea, feeling or intention you need to embrace from it? If so, what is it?

- What might God be inviting you to be, know, understand, feel or even do?

Be open to the quiet and don't feel pressured to come up with an answer.

Respond (*ORATIO*)

Take a few minutes to respond to God about this. What do you most want to say to God about this experience in Scripture?

Rest (*CONTEMPLATIO*)

Soak in the sort of life that is described in this passage. This is possible as we live "in Christ." How does that possibility strike you?

Spend a few minutes noticing the thoughts that have come to you. This may take the form of worship or simply resting in God's presence.

Trying It On (*INCARNATIO*)

Consider ways to choose Christ and Christ's love as the radio station playing in your head. If so, how might you think differently when you begin to worry about something? How might you view people differently? How might you think differently as you plan your day?

Embracing the New Self

Colossians 3:12-17

RELAX AND REFOCUS (*SILENCIO*)

Center yourself by breathing in and out. Relax your neck and take time to let your muscles relax.

Optional—If you need help focusing, consider this question: How would you most like to change?

READ (*LECTIO*)

Read the passage to yourself silently. Then read the notes below it about the key words and phrases. Consider how these details help your understanding of the passage. Then read the passage aloud slowly. Take time to let the words "fall on your ear."

REFLECT (*MEDITATIO*)

Questions and cues to help you reflect on the passage.

1. In the King James Version, "compassion" is translated "bowels of mercies." Adam Clarke commented on this strange-sounding phrase, saying, "Be merciful, not in act merely, but in spirit and affection. . . . Let your heart dictate to your hand; . . . let your tenderest feelings come in contact with the miseries of the distressed as soon as ever they present themselves."[1]

Colossians 3:12-17

¹²Therefore, as God's chosen people, holy and dearly loved, clothe your-selves with compassion, kindness, humility, gentleness and patience. **¹³*Bear with*** each other and forgive one another if any of you has a griev-ance against someone. Forgive as the Lord forgave you. **¹⁴**And over all these virtues put on love, which binds them all together in perfect unity.

¹⁵Let the peace of Christ ***rule*** in your hearts, since as members of one body you were called to peace. And be thankful. **¹⁶**Let the message of Christ ***dwell*** among you richly as you teach and ***admonish*** one another with all wisdom through psalms, hymns, and songs from the Spirit, singing to God with gratitude in your hearts. **¹⁷**And whatever you do, whether in word or deed, ***do it all in the name of*** the Lord Jesus, giving thanks to God the Father through him.

Bear with In other places, the verb *anechomai* (Strong's 430) is translated "put up with," but not here. This isn't about rolling your eyes in despair or cynicism, but treating others with generosity and tenderness. It means "to make allowances for the weaknesses of others."[2]

rule From *brabeuō* (Strong's 1017-1018), which means "to govern or act as an umpire."

dwell From *enoikeō* (Strong's 1774), which means "to inhabit."

admonish From *noutheteō* (Strong's 3560), "to put in mind; to caution or reprove gently; to warn."

do it all in the name of That is, on behalf of Jesus, in the presence and power of Jesus, doing things the way Jesus would do them.

Who do you know that seems to have compassion to that degree? If you can't think of anyone, when did Jesus seem to have this kind of compassion?

2. The following phrases from verses 16-17 give us clues about what it looks like to have Christ's peace rule us and Christ's message dwell in us. Paul, for example, sang while he was in jail (Acts 16:25).

How might you do the following things when, for example, you wash your car or eat a meal with relatives?

- Teach and admonish one another with all wisdom
- through psalms, hymns and songs from the Spirit,
- singing to God with gratitude in your hearts.
- Whatever you do, whether in word or deed, do it all in the name of the Lord Jesus,
- giving thanks to God the Father through him.

How would life be different if this was your normal routine?

3. Notice how often gratefulness is mentioned in verses 15, 16 and 17. Why do you think that quality is so central in "putting on Christ"?

4. *Scriptural connections: God's love for us.* Notice that the first paragraph (verses 12-14) begins with our being loved and ends with our becoming people who love others. The phrase "holy and dearly loved" is similar to 1 John 3:1: "See what great love the Father has lavished on us, that we should be called children of God! And that is what we are!" Receiving and embracing God's love initiates within us an organic response of love for others, of wanting to embrace compassion, kindness, humility, gentleness and patience.

Reflect on the invitation. Perhaps God is offering you an invitation in this passage to enlarge your understanding about something. What might that be? Read the passage again and then sit quietly for a few minutes, pondering these questions:

- What word or phrase stands out to you?
- Why do you think that is?
- Is there a word or phrase or idea that moves you? Why?

Reflect a little further. You may wish to read the passage again. Then consider:

- How does this passage connect with your life?

- Is there some idea, feeling or intention you need to embrace from it? If so, what is it?

- What might God be inviting you to be, know, understand, feel or even do?

Be open to the quiet and don't feel pressured to come up with an answer.

RESPOND (*ORATIO*)

Imagine for a moment that in your own funeral, someone says these words about you. Put your name in the blank.

_____ knew she/he was loved by God. ____ was so drenched with compassion, kindness, humility, gentleness and patience that it was as if _____ was wearing them like clothes.

_____ knew how to bear with people and forgive them the way Christ had forgiven him/her. Love characterized everything ____ did.

I often noticed that the peace of Christ was so strong in _____ that it seemed to permeate everything he/she did. He/she was always thanking people! What Jesus taught lived itself out in _____. We saw it as ____ expressed ideas with wisdom and was always going around with a song under his/her breath and a smile. I'm so glad that I knew ____ because I know Christ better from having known him/her. I'm so grateful to God for that glimpse of Jesus.

Take a few minutes to picture this. Then respond to God about this in prayer.

REST (*CONTEMPLATIO*)

Soak in this vision of yourself presented in the imaginary eulogy above. Why would God want this kind of life for you?

Spend a few minutes noticing the thoughts that have come to you. This may take the form of worship or simply resting in God's presence.

TRYING IT ON (*INCARNATIO*)

A way to clothe ourselves with character qualities such as compassion and humility is to practice spiritual disciplines that help people experiment with various versions of those virtues. For example, to try on humility, you might try speaking with simplicity (not always trying to have the last word, not always giving advice). To try on kindness or generosity, you might go out of your way for someone once a day. Ask God for an idea of how you might experiment with trying on compassion, kindness, humility, gentleness or patience.

20

Dying to Self

John 13:1-14

RELAX AND REFOCUS (*SILENCIO*)

Center yourself by breathing in and out. Relax your neck and take time to let your muscles relax.

Optional—If you wish, consider this quotation and the following question to focus your thoughts on today's passage:

> Death to self is about being crucified with Christ daily (Galatians 2:20). It is not to be confused with death *of* self, because God doesn't want to blot us out or make us disappear. God treasures each of us and respects us. Death *to* self is releasing the desire to have things my way and being open to how God leads me today.[1]

How do you respond to the idea of dying to self?

☐ Sounds too unselfish to me.

☐ This is puzzling.

☐ Sounds scary.

☐ Why would anyone want to do this?

☐ I have no idea how to do this.

☐ I don't know anyone who is "dying to self."

☐ This helps explain why I don't change.

☐ Other:_____

READ (*LECTIO*)

Read the passage to yourself. Then read the notes below it about the key words and phrases. Consider how these details affect your understanding of the story. Then read the passage aloud slowly. Take time to let the words "fall on your ear."

John 13:1-14

1It was **just before the Passover Festival**. Jesus knew that the hour had come for him to leave this world and go to the Father. Having loved his own who were in the world, he loved them to the end.

2The evening meal was in progress, and the devil had already prompted Judas, the son of Simon Iscariot, to betray Jesus. **3**Jesus knew that the Father had **put all things under his power**, and that he had come from God and was returning to God; **4**so he got up from the meal, **took off his outer clothing, and wrapped a towel around his waist**. **5**After that, he poured water into a basin and began to **wash his disciples' feet**, drying them with the towel that was wrapped around him.

6He came to Simon Peter, who said to him, "Lord, are you going to wash my feet?"

---

just before the Passover Festival Jesus was about to be arrested and crucified. This passage comes after the disciples had been arguing about who would be considered greatest (Luke 22:24-30). They had been discussing their rights, privileges or what they deserved.
put all things under his power In spite of this, Jesus chose the powerless role of a slave in this scene, and later the powerless role of a criminal executed on a cross.
took off his outer clothing, and wrapped a towel around his waist A slave dressed in this manner.
wash his disciples' feet Because most people walked and many wore sandals or went barefoot in those times, feet took a similar beating to what the tires of our cars experience.

> ⁷Jesus replied, "You do not realize now what I am doing, but later you will understand."
>
> ⁸"No," said Peter, "you shall never wash my feet."
>
> Jesus answered, "Unless I wash you, you have no part with me."
>
> ⁹"Then, Lord," Simon Peter replied, "not just my feet but my hands and my head as well!"
>
> ¹⁰Jesus answered, "Those who have had a bath need only to wash their feet; their whole body is clean. And you are clean, though not every one of you." ¹¹For he knew who was going to betray him, and that was why he said not every one was clean.
>
> ¹²When he had finished washing their feet, he put on his clothes and returned to his place. "Do you understand what I have done for you?" he asked them. ¹³"You call me 'Teacher' and 'Lord,' and rightly so, for that is what I am. ¹⁴Now that I, your Lord and Teacher, have washed your feet, you also should wash one another's feet."

REFLECT (*MEDITATIO*)

Questions and cues to help you enter into the story.

1. *Cultural background.* Washing feet was to the disciples as "emptying a slop bucket or chamber pot would be to us. The scene is backwards: A rabbi's disciples were supposed to render personal service for their teacher, but instead their teacher is serving them. Apparently no slave is there to do this work and not one of them has volunteered because the task is too lowly."² This may have been especially true because the disciples had just been arguing among themselves about who would be regarded as the greatest (Luke 22:24-27).

2. If you had been one of the disciples, how would you have felt when you saw Jesus coming toward you with the basin? When your teacher was actually washing your feet, how would you respond?

   • Turn your eyes away.

- Look at Jesus, who is perhaps smiling at you.
- Tense your shoulders because this is such a strange, even abhorrent experience.
- Feel embarrassed to be the center of attention.
- Other:_____

3. How do you think Judas felt when Jesus washed his feet? Judas was getting ready to betray Jesus to the authorities for thirty pieces of silver (verse 2).

   What was it like for Jesus to wash Judas's feet, knowing he was washing the feet of someone who was choosing to be his enemy and false friend?

4. *Fly on the wall cue: Picture Jesus' manner.* Based on what you know of Jesus, with what attitude did he most likely wash their feet? Here are some ideas based 1 Corinthians 13:4-7.

- Patience—he wasn't in a hurry.
- Kindness—he paid tender attention to any tough spots.
- Without envy or pride—he didn't congratulate himself for humility; nor was he trying to show them up.
- Not rude or self-seeking—he didn't make comments about their worn feet but treated each foot as part of someone he dearly loved.
- Not easily irritated—he didn't roll his eyes at impossible Peter!
- Always protects—maybe he prayed for each disciple as he washed their feet.
- Other:_____

5. *Glowing phrases.*

   "Jesus knew that the hour had come for him to leave this world and go to the Father. Having loved his own who were in the world, he loved them to the end" (verse 1). Selfless service such as washing people's feet is

not what most of us would do. Jesus was able to take the role of a slave because he knew who he was and knew his purpose ("he loved his own"). As we abide in Christ and live in God's companionship, God's self-giving love overflows out of us.

6. *Dying to self: Role in transformation.* This passage may seem like a strange fit for a section of meditations on transformation. It is included because transformation involves not only taking on the good and lovely character of Christ but also letting go of the things that plague us or distract us from following God. This could be summed up as the self-referenced life: self-absorbed, self-centered, self-seeking, self-interested. Dying to self is about letting go of self-referenced thinking and moving forward in the kingdom of God.

Reflect on the invitation. Read the passage aloud again. Picture what the scene would look like. Hear the words clearly.

- As you picture the passage, what moment or action is most real to you?
- As you watch the action unfold, what do you see? What does this cause you to think and feel?
- Why might God have caused that moment, word or phrase to stand out to you?
- What feeling do you come away with from this story?
- In what real life situation have you had that same feeling or thought or desire (even though the situation may be completely different)?

Reflect a little further.

- How does this passage connect with your life?
- Is there some idea, feeling or intention you need to embrace from it? If so, what is it?
- What might God be inviting you to be, know, understand, feel or even do?

Be open to the quiet and don't feel pressured to come up with an answer.

RESPOND (*ORATIO*)

Take a few minutes to respond to God about this.

If you have taken the role of a disciple and have imagined Jesus washing your feet, what do you want to say to Jesus?

REST (*CONTEMPLATIO*)

Soak in what has stood out to you in this passage and consider: How did Jesus' actions seem to you in this passage? What does Jesus' behavior tell you about what God is like?

Spend a few minutes noticing the thoughts that have come to you. This may take the form of worship or simply resting in God's presence.

TRYING IT ON (*INCARNATIO*)

Do some rudimentary task such as scrubbing your floor or sweeping your neighbor's driveway. Imagine for a moment that you are Jesus. With what kind of heart might Jesus do this?

A Huge Maturity Gap

Sometimes when I read a passage of Scripture, something in it—the behavior of the main character or a command in the passage—seems far beyond my own capabilities. It feels foreign to me. I feel that I could never do that. Maybe I don't even want to. One of those passages has been the story of Jesus washing his disciples' feet. I just don't have that kind of servant heart. When this happens it's tempting to feel inadequate and discouraged.

Don't let yourself fall into this trap. You don't need to make yourself the center of what you read. The passage is obviously not about you—although it may be a vision of the kind of person God is transforming you to be, slowly but surely. Confess that you are nothing like what the passage describes.

Then, if Jesus is involved in the biblical scene (and he always is, in one way or another), we can admire him. Worship him. Too often people think that Jesus is a lot like any of us, only nicer. But God is perfect love. The Trinity is wholly other. That means it's appropriate to respond in wonder and praise.

You might also consider what you read as a beautiful vision of life in the kingdom of God. This is the life God invites us into. Some of us are walking into it more slowly than others. As you gaze in wonder at how the kingdom of God works, you might long for the reality of God's kingdom "on earth as it is in heaven"—in you as it is in Christ.

21

Finding Courage
in the Storm

Mark 4:35-41

RELAX AND REFOCUS (*SILENCIO*)

Inhale and exhale a few times. Let go of distractions. Quiet your thoughts and open yourself to God. As you quiet yourself, you may wish to use the palms up, palms down method described in the introduction. Rest your hands in your lap, placing your hands palms down as a symbol of turning over any concerns you have. If a nagging thought arises, turn your hands palms up as a "symbol of your desire to receive from the Lord."[1] If you become distracted at any time during meditation, repeat the exercise.

Optional—This section is about facing fear. If you need help focusing, think of a time when God calmed your fears. What was that like for you? Recall the peace or settledness that you experienced.

READ (*LECTIO*)

Read the passage to yourself. Then read the notes below it about the key words and phrases. Consider how these details affect your understanding of the story. Then read the passage aloud slowly. Take time to let the words "fall on your ear."

Mark 4:35-41

35That day when evening came, he said to his disciples, "Let us go over to the other side." **36**Leaving the crowd behind, they took him along, just as he was, in the boat. There were also other boats with him. **37**A furious squall came up, and the waves broke over the boat, so that it was nearly swamped. **38**Jesus was in the stern, sleeping on a cushion. The disciples woke him and said to him, "Teacher, don't you care if we drown?"

39He got up, ***rebuked*** the wind and said to the waves, "Quiet! Be still!" Then the wind died down and it was completely calm.

40He said to his disciples, "Why are you so afraid? Do you still have no faith?"

41They were terrified and asked each other, "Who is this? Even the wind and the waves obey him!"

That day Jesus had been teaching, first the crowd and then just the disciples, all day long (Mark 4:1-2, 10, 34).
rebuked Reprimanded, ordered, commanded.

REFLECT (*MEDITATIO*)

Questions and cues to help you enter into the story.

1. *Fly on the wall cue: Picture the wind storm.* Imagine the disciples in a furious wind storm with their boat filling up with water. What might they have been doing?

   - Watching the other disciples trying to scoop the water out of the boat. No one is able to move well because the boat is tossing and the water is getting deeper. They're probably unable to see land because of the wind and rain.

   - Listening to the loud noise of the wind and the faint sound of voices trying to shout over it. They hear water heaving around in the boat.

- Smelling the sweat of friends working hard to try to keep the boat upright and bailing water.

- Feeling the waves possibly crashing in their face; feeling cold not only from the wind and rain, but also from the rising water in the boat.

In the midst of these sensations, what feelings might the disciples have had?

2. *Fly on the wall cue: Picture the moment after Jesus calmed the storm.* Imagine the disciples in this moment: "Then the wind died down and it was completely calm" (verse 39). They're able to stand up without holding on to something. The terrific noise is gone. The waves are calm.

   What might they have been feeling or thinking at this point?

3. *Fly on the wall cue: Picture Jesus speaking.* Consider the many different ways Jesus could have said, "Why are you so afraid? Do you still have no faith?" People sometimes assume Jesus was scolding the disciples, as if he thought they should have known that he could command the wind and the waves. But they had no reason to know that. For him to have scolded or even teased them would have been demeaning and very out of character for Jesus.

   What are the other possibilities for how Jesus said these words?

   - Jesus was reassuring them to let go of fear, to always trust him.

   - Jesus was inviting them to think of him as someone they could always trust.

   - Jesus was grinning, as if to say, "See? You can trust me—even with the wind!"

   - Jesus was challenging them to piece together what they had just seen him do with his other miracles of nature such as his turning the water into wine. What did these miracles tell them about who he really was?

   - Other:_____

4. *Fly on the wall cue*: *Picture the scene using Rembrandt's painting,* The Storm on the Sea of Galilee.[2] This painting represents the variety of the disciples' responses well. Some are frantically trying to keep the boat afloat; others are upset and perhaps even yelling at Jesus; still others are cowering in fear; one poor disciple is heaving over the side.[3]

Do you see yourself in one or more of the disciples in the painting? If so, what are you feeling?

What do you want to say to Jesus at this point?

Rembrandt often inserted himself in his paintings. It is supposed that he put himself in this painting as the man kneeling in front of Jesus.

Reflect on the invitation. Read the passage aloud again. Picture what the scene would look like. Hear the words clearly.

- As you picture the passage, what moment, action or phrase stands out to you?

- As you watch the action, what do you see? What does this make you think or feel?

- Why might God have made that moment, word or phrase stand out to you?

- What feeling does this story leave you with?

   Reflect a little further.

- How does this passage connect with your life?

- Is there some idea, feeling or intention you need to embrace from it? If so, what is it?

- What might God be inviting you to be, know, understand, feel or even do?

Be open to the quiet and don't feel pressured to come up with an answer.

Respond (*ORATIO*)

The disciples responded to this event with terror, asking each other who Jesus really was. Jesus wanted them to let go of their fear and trust him (verse 40).

Take a few minutes to respond to Jesus himself about what you experienced in this passage. What do you most want to say to him?

You may wish to write your prayer down, use colored pens to describe your feelings or to draw the scene as you see it. You may want to ask God questions (the answers to which may come to you later).

Rest (*CONTEMPLATIO*)

Soak in what has stood out to you in this passage and consider: How did Jesus (or Jesus' actions) seem to you in this passage? What does this tell you about what God is like?

Spend a few minutes noticing the thoughts that have come to you. This may take the form of worship or simply resting in God's presence.

Trying It On (*INCARNATIO*)

Look for moments in your life where you are afraid—maybe afraid to step out and help someone, afraid to risk something, afraid of what others will say if you do the right thing—and ask Jesus to reassure you to trust him.

Diving Board Lectio

A student once told me that he liked having some rudimentary background study, historical context and scriptural background because it prevented what he called "diving board lectio." He was referring to the way some people may jump off into the deep end—an unrelated direction which is far afield from the meaning of the passage. (Often this is a way to manipulate the text to say what the person wants to hear!) The practice of lectio divina—waiting for a word or phrase to stand out—is not a superficial treatment of Scripture. This book assumes that study (left brain) and meditation (right brain) work better together.

Lectio divina is not about shutting down the intellect. It is true that it came about in an era when the common person had little access to books and was not capable of scholarship. In the beginning it was often led by monks, many of whom were scholars who assumed that much more than intellect comes into play.

In that pre-Enlightenment era, before knowledge became so bifurcated into knowledge by reason and knowledge by experience, people understood that the intellect and the spirit were not enemies. Instead they work together. They also understood that, as Dallas Willard once wrote, "The Word of God as Scripture is not a book for scholars, but for plain people. It speaks to plain people. We must leave room for that."[1]

So lectio divina is not about trying to think up stuff. On the contrary, it's about avoiding the tendency to mold the text into what we think we need to hear and instead being open to the Holy Spirit.

Moving Through
a Fearful Journey

Psalm 91

RELAX AND REFOCUS (*SILENCIO*)

Inhale and exhale a few times. Let go of distractions. Quiet your thoughts and open yourself to God.

Optional—You may wish to begin by considering this question. According to Tom Wright, the most frequent command in the Bible is "Don't be afraid," or "Fear not."[1] Why would that command be so important? What does fear keep us from doing?

READ (*LECTIO*)

Read the passage to yourself silently. Then read the notes below it about the key words and phrases. Consider how these details help your understanding of the passage. Then read the passage aloud slowly. Take time to let the words "fall on your ear."

REFLECT (*MEDITATIO*)

Questions and cues to help you reflect on the passage.

1. *Fly on the wall cue: Picture a dangerous journey.* Some commentators believe this psalm is about a "traveler who must go in dangerous

Psalm 91 (NRSV)

¹You who live in the shelter of the Most High,
   who abide in the shadow of the Almighty,
²will say to the LORD, "My refuge and my fortress;
   my God, in whom I trust."
³For he will deliver you from the snare of the *fowler*
   and from the deadly pestilence;
⁴he will cover you with his *pinions*,
   and under his wings you will find refuge;
   his faithfulness is a shield and *buckler*.
⁵You will not fear the terror of the night,
   or the arrow that flies by day,
⁶or the pestilence that stalks in darkness,
   or the destruction that wastes at noonday.

⁷A thousand may fall at your side,
   ten thousand at your right hand,
   but it will not come near you.
⁸You will only look with your eyes
   and see the punishment of the wicked.

⁹Because you have made the LORD your refuge,
   the Most High your dwelling place,
¹⁰no evil shall befall you,
   no *scourge* come near your tent.

¹¹For he will command his angels concerning you
   to guard you in all your ways.

---

fowler A shooter or trapper of wild birds.
pinions The outer part of a bird's wing, including the flight feathers.
buckler A small round shield held by a handle at arm's length.
scourge A plague or tormentor.

> ¹²On their hands they will bear you up,
>   so that you will not dash your foot against a stone.
> ¹³You will tread on the lion and the adder,
>   the young lion and the serpent you will trample under foot.
>
> ¹⁴Those who love me, I will deliver;
>   I will protect those who know my name.
> ¹⁵When they call to me, I will answer them;
>   I will be with them in trouble,
>   I will rescue them and honor them.
> ¹⁶With long life I will satisfy them,
>   and show them my salvation.

places." Travel in ancient times was risky, but this traveler, though "constantly beset with threats," is experiencing a "safe journey."[2] The psalmist describes a journey fraught with hazards: hunters, diseases, flying arrows and wild animals. Death was striking people all around. Dangers popped up both day and night (verses 5-6).

Sometimes we think of the psalms as sweet, pleasant little poems composed in a cozy room by dim light. Nothing could be further from the truth. The psalms are based in real life-threatening situations. Psalm 91 resembles the classic work *The Pilgrim's Progress* with its constant threats. It speaks to us in our lowest moments.

2. What activity now or in the past have you undertaken that is or was fraught with hazards? Was it finishing college, starting a new job, becoming a parent, facing surgery or facing a difficult financial time? What phrase in verses 3-13 best describes the hazards of that journey?

As you look back now, how might God have been taking care of you?

• Kept you from greater harm

- Sent people to guard or encourage you
- Showed you the way forward
- Other:_____

3. *Majesty and intimacy.* Verses 1 and 2 combine the majesty of God (describing him as "Most High," "Almighty" and "Lord") with God's personal protection in the intimacy of God's shadow ("my refuge and my fortress"). This combination refutes both the familiar "God is my buddy" attitude as well as the idea that God is a faraway deity who has better things to think about than mere human beings. God is both majestic and intimate—transcendent and immanent—all in the same moment.

Which do you find more difficult to think about: God's closeness to you or God's divine majesty?

Try saying verses 1-2 aloud and embracing both ideas at the same time.

4. *The surprising speech of God.* Now and then in the Psalms, God seems to abruptly interrupt the psalmist. Verses 14-16 is "the direct speech of Yahweh in the form of a decree of assurance." As Walter Brueggemann explains, the speech overflows with commitment:

> "I will deliver, I will protect, I will answer, I will be with him, I will rescue, [I will] honor him, I will satisfy, [I will] show." The promise articulated in the human assurance (vv. 1-3) is now verified in divine speech (vv. 14-16). . . . The last word is not spoken *by* us, but *to* us.[3]

- Consider the tone of voice God might use in saying verses 14-16 to someone: bold, gentle, quiet, thundering, certain. Any of these is possible.

- Perhaps God would place great emphasis on the repetitive word "will," or perhaps on the verb that follows "will" (*deliver, protect* and so on). God would no doubt know what tone is needed in each moment.

- Try reading these verses aloud and use the tone God might use that you most need in this moment:

> ¹⁴Those who love me, I will deliver;
>   I will protect those who know my name.

> ¹⁵When they call to me, I will answer them;
>   I will be with them in trouble,
>   I will rescue them and honor them.

> ¹⁶With long life I will satisfy them,
>   and show them my salvation.

Reflect on the invitation. Perhaps God is offering you an invitation in this passage to increase your understanding about God's own self or about something that has happened (or is happening) to you. What might that be? Read the passage again and then sit quietly for a few minutes, pondering these questions:

- What word or phrase stands out to you?

- Why do you think that is?

Reflect a little further. You may wish to read the passage again. Then consider:

- How does this passage connect with your life?

- Is there some idea, feeling or intention you need to embrace from it? If so, what is it?

- What might God be inviting you to be, know, understand, feel or even do?

Be open to the quiet and don't feel pressured to come up with an answer.

RESPOND (*ORATIO*)

Take a few minutes to respond to God about this. What do you most want to say to God about this experience in Scripture?

If you wish, pray the psalm back to God, inserting "Thank you that . . ." or "I am glad that . . ." It might start out something like: "Thank you that I live in your sheltering protection, Oh Most High, and that I abide in your Almighty shadow. I am glad to say to you, 'My refuge . . .'"

Rest (*CONTEMPLATIO*)

Soak in what has stood out to you in this passage and consider: How did God (or God's actions) seem to you in this passage?

Spend a few minutes noticing the thoughts that have come to you. This may take the form of worship or simply resting in God's presence.

Trying It On (*INCARNATIO*)

Read or listen to the news. When you hear about someone in a dangerous situation, pray this psalm for the people caught in the situation.

Seeing Jesus in Anger, Grief and Mercy

Mark 3:1-6

RELAX AND REFOCUS (*SILENCIO*)

Inhale and exhale a few times. Let go of distractions. Quiet your thoughts and open yourself to God.

Optional—To orient yourself toward today's meditation, consider a time when you have been frustrated or grieved over a situation.

READ (*LECTIO*)

Read the passage to yourself. Then read the notes below it about the key words and phrases. Consider how these details affect your understanding of the story. Then read the passage aloud slowly. Take time to let the words "fall on your ear."

REFLECT (*MEDITATIO*)

Questions and cues to help you enter into the story.

1. *Scriptural connections: Jesus and the law.* In Matthew's account we find a few more details. "Looking for a reason to bring charges against Jesus, they asked him, 'Is it lawful to heal on the Sabbath?' He said to them, 'If any of you has a sheep and it falls into a pit on the Sabbath,

Mark 3:1-6

¹Another time Jesus went into the synagogue, and a man with a shriveled hand was there. ²Some of **them** were looking for a reason to accuse Jesus, so they watched him closely to see if he would heal him **on the Sabbath**. ³Jesus said to the man with the shriveled hand, "Stand up in front of everyone."

⁴Then Jesus asked them, "Which is lawful on the Sabbath: to do good or to do evil, to save life or to kill?" But they remained silent.

⁵He looked around at them in **anger** and, deeply distressed at their stubborn hearts, said to the man, "Stretch out your hand." He stretched it out, and his hand was completely restored. ⁶Then the Pharisees went out and began to **plot with the Herodians how they might kill Jesus**.

---

them The Pharisees (see Mark 2:24).

on the Sabbath The Pharisees considered healing to be work, which was prohibited on the Sabbath. They considered Jesus a disrespectful renegade preacher.

anger The Greek word, *orgē* (Strong's 3709), is often translated "furious," indicating violent passion and indignation.

Herodians A political group that supported Herod as king of the Jews. Most Jews saw Herod as an imposter, since he was Idumean and not truly Jewish. This was the same King Herod who had John the Baptist beheaded (Mark 6:22-29).

plot . . . how they might kill Jesus The Pharisees' hypervigilance for the law turned to making violent plans to kill Jesus. Jesus' anger, on the contrary, didn't lead to violence, but healing.

---

will you not take hold of it and lift it out? How much more valuable is a person than a sheep! Therefore it is lawful to do good on the Sabbath'" (Matthew 12:10-12).

In that time as well as today, some people liked to portray Jesus as a rebellious figure, but that was not his aim. Jesus knew the Mosaic Law and obeyed it. It was the leaders' interpretation of the law that he disagreed with.

Jesus appealed to the law to show that healing the distressed man was right and good:

- "When you come upon your enemy's ox or donkey going astray, you shall bring it back. When you see the donkey of one who hates you lying under its burden and you would hold back from setting it free, you must help to set it free" (Exodus 23:4-5 NRSV).

- "You shall do the same with a neighbor's donkey; you shall do the same with a neighbor's garment; and you shall do the same with anything else that your neighbor loses and you find. You may not withhold your help. You shall not see your neighbor's donkey or ox fallen on the road and ignore it; you shall help to lift it up" (Deuteronomy 22:3-4 NRSV).

- "Do not withhold good from those to whom it is due, when it is in your power to do it" (Proverbs 3:27 NRSV).

It's quite possible that Jesus cared about the Pharisees' relationship with God and knew that withholding help can be destructive. Do you think that's true? If so, how does withholding help affect our relationship with God or our character? If not, why not?

2. *Reason for Jesus' anger.* Jesus was angry because he was "deeply distressed at their stubborn hearts" ("grieved at their hardness of heart," NRSV). He mourned the condition of the hearts of the Pharisees as spiritual leaders of the Jews. (It appears that they may have planted the disabled man to trap Jesus. For instance, compare Luke 6:7: "The Pharisees and the teachers of the law were looking for a reason to accuse Jesus, so they watched him closely to see if he would heal on the Sabbath.") The trajectory of Jesus' emotions and accompanying actions seems to have been first anger, then grief and finally mercy.

Why do people usually get angry? For example, perhaps they want to have things their way and their will is thwarted. Or perhaps they've been rejected or treated unjustly.

How do Jesus' reasons for anger compare with the reasons that most people get angry?

3. People generally become the worst version of themselves when they're angry. At times, they become someone they themselves wouldn't even recognize. When Jesus was angry, he still acted like himself. He often healed people; even in his anger he healed someone. He was often grieved by people's hardness of heart; in anger he was grieved. Jesus asked his question ("Which is lawful . . .") and then said nothing. The text notes his anger, but his only words and actions were to heal the man with the shriveled hand.

How did Jesus act differently in anger than most people do?

4. *Fly on the wall cue: Picture the synagogue at Capernaum.* This was the home synagogue of Peter, Andrew, James and John and the scene of many dramatic events. Jesus had healed a demon-possessed man there (Mark 1:21-28). After he healed Peter's mother-in-law, the whole town of Capernaum gathered at the door and Jesus healed them (Mark 1:29-34). A few months after the incident with the man with the shriveled hand, Jesus resurrected the daughter of Jairus, the leader of the synagogue, and healed the woman with the twelve-year flow of blood (Mark 5:21-43).

Reflect on the invitation. As you read the passage again, imagine yourself as a fly on the wall. What do you see, hear, taste, touch or smell? You may find yourself identifying with particular people. How do you think these people felt?

- *The Pharisees* were "back to the Bible" people. They thought Jesus wasn't paying attention to God's laws (although it was actually the additional details they had added that he ignored).

- *The disciples*—several of whom probably knew everyone in the room, since this was their hometown.

- *The man with the shriveled hand*—especially if he was coerced or even paid to do this to provoke Jesus. Before this he would have struggled to find work, etc.

- *The man's wife or family* (if he had one).

Reflect a little further.

- How does this passage connect with your life?

- Is there some idea, feeling or intention you need to embrace from it? If so, what is it?

- What might God be inviting you to be, know, understand, feel or even do?

Be open to the quiet and don't feel pressured to come up with an answer.

RESPOND (*ORATIO*)

Take a few minutes to respond to God about this. What do you most want to say to Jesus about how he behaved that day?

If you have questions for Jesus about his anger or the anger you experience at times, ask him those questions.

REST (*CONTEMPLATIO*)

Soak in what has stood out to you in this passage and consider: How did Jesus seem to you in this passage? Consider that Jesus is a snapshot of God (the "exact representation of his being," Hebrews 1:3). What do Jesus' words, feelings and actions in this scene tell you about what God is like?

Spend a few minutes noticing the thoughts that have come to you. This may take the form of worship or simply resting in God's presence.

TRYING IT ON (*INCARNATIO*)

Pick a situation that annoys or frustrates you. What is there to grieve about in this situation? Tell God about your grief. How do you think God responds to your grief?

Moving from
Cynicism to Hope

Psalm 27

You may wish to meditate on this psalm over two days (verses 1-6, 7-14) or over four days (verses 1-3, 4-6, 7-10, 11-14).

RELAX AND REFOCUS (*SILENCIO*)

Center yourself by breathing in and out. Relax your neck and take time to let your muscles relax.

Optional—Consider this question to focus your thoughts on today's passage: When have you been set free from a fear, frustration or discouragement?

READ (*LECTIO*)

Read the passage to yourself silently. Then read the notes below it about the key words and phrases. Consider how these details help your understanding of the passage. Then read the passage aloud slowly. Take time to let the words "fall on your ear."

Psalm 27

1The LORD is my *light* and my *salvation*—
     whom shall I fear?
The LORD is the *stronghold* of my life—
     of whom shall I be afraid?

2When the wicked advance against me
     to devour me,
it is my enemies and my foes
     who will stumble and fall.
3Though an army besiege me,
     my heart will not fear;
though war break out against me,
     even then I will be confident.

4One thing I ask from the LORD,
     this only do I seek:
that I may dwell in the house of the LORD
     all the days of my life,
to *gaze on the beauty of the Lord*
     and to seek him in his temple.
5For in the day of trouble
     he will keep me safe in his dwelling;
he will hide me in the shelter of his sacred tent
     and set me high upon a rock.

---

light In Scripture, light usually refers to power, truth and love.[1]
salvation The Hebrew word, *yesha* (Strong's 3468), refers to liberty, deliverance, prosperity and safety (deliverance from almost any kind of evil, material or spiritual).[2] Theologically, it denotes the whole process by which we are delivered from everything that interferes with our enjoyment of God's highest blessings.[3]
stronghold A refuge, place of defense or military fortress.
gaze on the beauty of the Lord Brueggemann describes this as "encountering the life-giving divine presence."[4]

⁶Then my head will be **exalted**
    above the enemies who surround me;
at his sacred tent I will sacrifice with shouts of joy;
    I will sing and make music to the LORD.

⁷Hear my voice when I call, LORD;
    be merciful to me and answer me.
⁸My heart says of you, "Seek his face!"
    Your face, LORD, I will seek.
⁹Do not **hide your face from me**,
    do not turn your servant away in anger;
    you have been my helper.
Do not reject me or forsake me,
    God my Savior.
¹⁰Though my father and mother forsake me,
    the LORD will receive me.
¹¹Teach me your way, LORD;
    lead me in a straight path
    because of my oppressors.
¹²Do not turn me over to the desire of my foes,
    for false witnesses rise up against me,
    spouting malicious accusations.

¹³I remain confident of this:
    I will see the goodness of the LORD
    in the **land of the living**.
¹⁴Wait for the LORD;
    be strong and take heart
    and wait for the LORD.

---

exalted Lifted up—an indication of victory.
hide your face from me Asking God not to withdraw his divine presence.
because of my oppressors Perhaps the psalmist's enemies diverted him from the straight path.
land of the living That is, during the psalmist's own lifetime.

REFLECT (*MEDITATIO*)

Questions and cues to help you reflect on the passage.

1. Psalm 27 (like Psalms 23 and 91) is a "Song of Confidence."[5] What words do you find in Psalm 27 that indicate despair or confidence? List them below.

DESPAIR	CONFIDENCE & HOPE
fear, afraid	salvation

2. When have you experienced God in your daily life as power, truth or love?

3. When have you experienced God as salvation from sickness, internal turmoil, difficulties with other people or authorities?

4. In the book of Psalms, waiting is not a passive, impatient moment full of frustration. It is an active waiting, full of hoping and believing. In fact, the words *wait* and *hope* often appear together (Psalm 39:7; 130:5). See especially Psalm 62:5: "Yes, my soul, find rest in God; my hope comes from him." Such hopeful waiting is expectant, with eyes wide open to the possibility of God acting at any moment.

With that in mind, how might you paraphrase verse 14?

Wait for the LORD;
> be strong and take heart
> and *wait* for the LORD.

Reflect on the invitation. Perhaps God is offering you an invitation in this passage to enlarge your understanding about something. What might that be? Read the passage again and then sit quietly for a few minutes, pondering these questions:

• What word or phrase stands out to you?

• Why do you think that is?

Reflect a little further. You may wish to read the passage again. Then consider:

- How does this passage connect with your life?

- Is there some idea, feeling or intention you need to embrace from it? If so, what is it?

- What might God be inviting you to be, know, understand, feel or even do?

Be open to the quiet and don't feel pressured to come up with an answer.

RESPOND (*ORATIO*)

Take a few minutes to respond to God about this. What do you most want to say to God about this experience in Scripture?

REST (*CONTEMPLATIO*)

Sit or stand a little taller and exhale in confidence. Soak in what has stood out to you in this passage and consider: How may God want to give you confidence today?

Spend a few minutes noticing the thoughts that have come to you. This may take the form of worship or simply resting in God's presence.

TRYING IT ON (*INCARNATIO*)

When you are alone (hiking may be ideal), say verse 1 to God. If it feels comfortable, put your whole body into it. For example:

(Raise your arms) "You are my light—power—and deliverance from what plagues me!"

(Put your hands on your hips in determination) "Whom shall I fear?"

(Raise your arms again) "You are the stronghold of my life!" (clench your fists)

(Put your hands on your hips again) "Of whom shall I be afraid?"

Continue in this manner if you wish. Be sure to include verse 3: "Yet will I be confident!"

What If Nothing Comes to Me?

Don't be concerned if nothing comes to you as you reflect on the Bible passage. Scripture meditation is not something you can control. Let God engineer it. As Thelma Hall writes, "We will never be 'in charge' in prayer if it is real."[1] The results may vary because much of the way Scripture communicates is by offering new facts, engaging stories and cleverly worded insights. What God imparts to us in meditation usually impacts the core of who we are.

Perhaps silence makes you uncomfortable. Gradually you may learn to welcome silence, understanding that it is a time of great fertility and growth, not of emptiness. Silence cultivates vulnerability toward God, because silence is an outward form of inward surrender. Being able to quiet yourself is the secret to hearing God well in meditation. Dallas Willard put it this way: "Nine-tenths of meditation is ignoring things, letting stuff go. It's the art of purposefully allowing stuff to drop off."[2]

Madeleine L'Engle compared meditation to planting onion bulbs in the ground. "They go down into the ground into silence, and they stay there in the silence and in the dark. And then these little green shoots come up. I think it is the same way with us spiritually, putting things down in the dark and letting them grow."[3]

So if nothing comes to you, simply cherish the time of Scripture meditation as time spent with God. You have not wasted time. You have tasted what it means to abide in Christ (John 15:4-10). The silence is not empty. God is full and present and you have rested secure in divine love.

Hearing God in the Midst of Discouragement

1 Kings 19:3-18

You may want to do this meditation in two or more sittings.

RELAX AND REFOCUS (*SILENCIO*)

Inhale and exhale a few times. Relax your neck and move it around. Then let your arms go limp and relax your legs and ankles. Quiet your thoughts and open yourself to God.

Optional—After you've quieted yourself, ask yourself the following question to help focus your thoughts for meditation on today's passage: When, if ever, have you felt like saying, "I have had enough, Lord"? If you haven't felt that way, what experience could possibly bring on those feelings?

READ (*LECTIO*)

Read the passage to yourself. Then read the notes below it about the key words and phrases. Consider how these details affect your understanding of the story. Then read the passage aloud slowly. Take time to let the words "fall on your ear."

1 Kings 19:3-18

³Elijah **was afraid** and ran for his life. When he came to Beersheba in Judah, he left his servant there, ⁴while he himself went a day's journey into the wilderness. He came to a broom bush, sat down under it and prayed that he might die. "I have had enough, LORD," he said. "Take my life; I am no better than my ancestors." ⁵Then he lay down under the bush and fell asleep.

All at once an angel touched him and said, "Get up and eat." ⁶He looked around, and there by his head was some **bread** baked over hot coals, and a jar of water. He ate and drank and then lay down again.

⁷The **angel of the LORD** came back a second time and touched him and said, "Get up and eat, for the journey is too much for you." ⁸So he got up and ate and drank. Strengthened by that food, he **traveled forty days and forty nights** until he reached **Horeb**, the mountain of God. ⁹There he went into a cave and spent the night.

And the word of the LORD came to him: "What are you doing here, Elijah?"

¹⁰He replied, "I have been very zealous for the LORD God Almighty. The Israelites have rejected your covenant, torn down your altars, and put your

was afraid Ahab and Jezebel, monarchs of Israel, worshiped Baal, a foreign god that Elijah prophesied against. Elijah had challenged the prophets of Baal to a contest in which Elijah proved God's power by calling down fire from heaven to consume his sacrifice. Baal's prophets got no response from their god, lost the contest and were killed (1 Kings 18:18-46).

bread These loaves of bread would have been flat. This substantive food fueled Elijah for forty days on his two hundred mile journey.

angel of the LORD The "angel of the LORD" is the one who appeared to Hagar to help her in the wilderness, to Abraham to keep him from sacrificing Isaac, to Moses in the burning bush, to Gideon in the winepress, to Manoah's wife to predict the birth of Samson and to Balaam on his donkey (Genesis 16:7-11; 22:11-19; Exodus 3:2; Numbers 22:22-35; Judges 13:3-21).

traveled forty days and forty nights Elijah fled the length of Israel from north to south (about ninety miles). Then he fled to Mt. Horeb in the southern tip of Arabia (two to three hundred more miles, depending on the route).[1]

Horeb another name for Mt. Sinai, where God had conversed with Moses centuries earlier. It's possible Elijah intended to imitate Moses's spectacular meetings with God (Exodus 24:15-18; 33:17-23).

prophets to death with the sword. I am the ***only one left***, and now they are trying to kill me too."

¹¹The LORD said, "Go out and stand on the mountain in the presence of the LORD, for the LORD is about to pass by."

Then a great and powerful wind tore the mountains apart and shattered the rocks before the LORD, but the LORD was not in the wind. After the wind there was an earthquake, but the LORD was not in the earthquake. ¹²After the earthquake came a fire, but the LORD was not in the fire. And after the fire came a ***gentle whisper***. ¹³When Elijah heard it, he pulled his cloak over his face and went out and stood at the mouth of the cave.

Then a voice said to him, "What are you doing here, Elijah?"

¹⁴He replied, "I have been very zealous for the LORD God Almighty. The Israelites have rejected your covenant, torn down your altars, and put your prophets to death with the sword. I am the ***only one left***, and now they are trying to kill me too."

¹⁵The LORD said to him, "Go back the way you came, and go to the Desert of Damascus. When you get there, ***anoint Hazael*** king over Aram. ¹⁶Also, ***anoint Jehu*** son of Nimshi king over Israel, and ***anoint Elisha*** son of Shaphat from Abel Meholah to succeed you as prophet. ¹⁷Jehu will put to death any who escape the sword of Hazael, and Elisha will put to death any who escape the sword of Jehu. ¹⁸Yet I reserve ***seven thousand*** in Israel—all whose knees have not bowed down to Baal and whose mouths have not kissed him."

---

only one left Jezebel had ordered the death of all the Lord's prophets (1 Kings 18:4).
gentle whisper Sometimes translated "sound of sheer silence" (NRSV).
anoint To set aside for a special purpose. One of a prophet's many duties.
Hazael The king of Syria, which would come against the northern kingdom of Israel, cleansing it from "without."
Jehu Jehu would be the new king of Israel who would cleanse Israel from "within." Anointing Hazael and Jehu assured Elijah that God was not letting the northern kingdom of Israel continue in a state of depravity.
Elisha Elisha would succeed Elijah and continue Elijah's prophetic work, calling Israel to obedience to God and performing miracles.
seven thousand Besides these, Elijah seemed to have forgotten about the one hundred prophets of God that Obadiah told Elijah about (1 Kings 18:4).

Reflect (*MEDITATIO*)

Questions and cues to help you enter into the story.

1. Elijah's fear seems puzzling. He previously stood up to Jezebel and Ahab (1 Kings 17:1; 18:17-40), but has suddenly became afraid of them. After he called down fire from heaven, Elijah would have been something of a celebrity in Israel. If he fled only because he was afraid of Jezebel, he could have easily fled to Judah to be safe with King Jehoshaphat. Instead Elijah fled all the way to Beersheba (farther south of Judah), and intended to go farther.

   Perhaps his fearful escape transitioned into a *pilgrimage*. He went on from Beersheba and headed for Mt. Sinai, where Moses had his well-known interaction with God. Was Elijah hoping for a similar encounter? The cave (verse 13) recalls the "hole in the rock" where Yahweh appeared to Moses (Exodus 33:17-23).

   Besides fear, why else might Elijah have fled?

   - Emotional lows can follow emotional highs (such as defeating the prophets of Baal).

   - He felt alone without any other prophets of God.

   - He was burned out; this was the last straw.

   - He had hoped that Ahab and Jezebel would give in, but they hadn't.

   - Other:_____

2. Our familiarity with a biblical account can numb us to the severity of the circumstances. Put yourself in Elijah's place and consider how you would respond to the following experiences.

   Rank these from 1-4, with 1 being the one that would have been most draining for you.

   ____ receiving a death threat

   ____ feeling suicidal

    ___ making a long journey on foot

    ___ encountering an angel

3. Which of the details about the angel's service to Elijah is most meaningful to you?

   - The angel respected Elijah's need for rest and made it possible.

   - The angel provided what appears to have been a prepared meal ("cake of bread baked over hot coals").

   - The meal the angel provided was substantial enough to sustain Elijah for forty days.

   - The angel's provision was simple: a few words and plain but substantial food.

4. Although God knew about Elijah's troubles, God still asked, "What are you doing here, Elijah?" In fact, God asked this twice (verses 9, 13), before and after Elijah's experience. How might this have been helpful to Elijah?

   - Speaking directly to God is important.

   - Putting our thoughts and feelings into audible words sometimes helps clarify problems.

   - Talking about something and feeling heard often provides relief.

   - Being asked twice helps us get beyond our go-to, no-brainer answer and think more deeply.

   - Other:_____

5. Part of how God responded to the discouraged prophet was to give him more work to do, including the anointing of a successor, Elisha. With Elisha at his side, it would have been hard for Elijah to ever feel again like he was the "only one left."

Has there been a time when you felt lonely, but God provided you with an unexpected source of joy and companionship? If so, when?

6. Many people find this description of Elijah reassuring: "Elijah was a human being, even as we are. He prayed earnestly that it would not rain, and it did not rain on the land for three and a half years. Again he prayed, and the heavens gave rain, and the earth produced its crops" (James 5:17-18).

How is this reassuring?

- Elijah prayed and was heard.

- Elijah heard God speaking to him even when he was "dissolving into a mass of righteous self-pity."[2]

- Hearing God is not rocket science.

7. *Fly on the wall cue: Picture Elijah under the tree.* Wearing a garment of haircloth and a wide belt, Elijah collapsed under a solitary broom bush in the desert. A broom bush is a large shrub that can grow up to thirteen feet high.[3] In the middle of a barren, treeless wilderness with animals and strange rock formations he found a shelter where there was usually none.

Elijah's mental and emotional state resembled that of someone standing on a bridge planning to jump. The angel saw Elijah and offered him water, food and rest.

Reflect on the invitation. Read the passage aloud again. Picture what the various scenes would look like.

- Elijah sitting under the tree.

- God providing Elijah tender mercies: sleep, food and sympathy.

- Elijah running off to an even more remote place to seek God.

- Elijah watching the great and powerful wind tearing the mountain apart and shattering the rocks, the earthquake and the fire. Then at last the gentle whisper.

- Elijah equipped with what he needed to return home.

As you picture the passage, what moment, action or phrase stands out to you? Or as you watch the action, what do you see?

- What does this make you think and feel?
- Why might God have caused that moment, word or phrase to stand out to you?

Reflect a little further.

- How does this passage connect with your life?
- Is there some idea, feeling or intention you need to embrace from it? If so, what is it?
- What might God be inviting you to know, understand, feel or do?
- What needs do you sense God asking you to surrender?

Be open to the quiet and don't feel pressured to come up with an answer.

RESPOND (*ORATIO*)

Take a few minutes to respond to God about this. What do you most want to say to God about this experience in Scripture?

REST (*CONTEMPLATIO*)

Soak in the scene, phrase, feeling or interaction that has stood out to you in this passage and consider: How did God (or God's actions) seem to you in this passage? What does this tell you about what God is like?

Spend a few minutes noticing the thoughts that have come to you. This may take the form of worship or simply resting in God's presence.

TRYING IT ON (*INCARNATIO*)

Make your own pilgrimage to a place where you have interacted with God before or that seems sacred to you for some reason. In that place, ask God to help you further let go of fear, frustration and discouragement.

26

Being Freed from Infirmities

Luke 13:10-17

RELAX AND REFOCUS (*SILENCIO*)

Inhale and exhale a few times. Let go of distractions. Quiet your thoughts and open yourself to God.

Optional—Consider someone you would like to see set free in some way.

READ (*LECTIO*)

Read the passage to yourself. Then read the notes below it about the key words and phrases. Consider how these details affect your understanding of the story. Then read the passage aloud slowly. Take time to let the words "fall on your ear."

REFLECT (*MEDITATIO*)

Questions and cues to help you enter into the story.

1. *Fly on the wall cue: The setting is Judea, not Galilee.* Jesus had healed people on the Sabbath before in Galilee, but this healing occurred in Judea. Rules were observed more strictly in Judea because Jerusalem was there, which meant many religious officials were nearby ("all his adversaries," verse 17). Also, this event occurred in the last six months

Luke 13:10-17 (ESV)

¹⁰Now he was teaching in one of the synagogues on the Sabbath. ¹¹And behold, there was a woman who had had a **disabling spirit** for eighteen years. She was bent over and could not fully straighten herself. ¹²When Jesus saw her, he called her over and said to her, "Woman, you are **freed** from your disability." ¹³And he laid his hands on her, and immediately she was made straight, and she glorified God. ¹⁴But the ruler of the synagogue, indignant because Jesus had healed on the Sabbath, said to the people, "There are six days in which work ought to be done. Come on those days and be healed, and not on the Sabbath day." ¹⁵Then the Lord answered him, "You hypocrites! Does not each of you on the Sabbath untie his ox or his donkey from the manger and lead it away to water it? ¹⁶And ought not this woman, a daughter of Abraham whom Satan bound for eighteen years, **be loosed** from this bond on the Sabbath day?" ¹⁷As he said these things, all his adversaries were put to shame, and all the people rejoiced at all the glorious things that were done by him.

---

disabling spirit Literally, a "spirit of weakness." As N. T. Wright explains, coming from Dr. Luke this probably meant that "nobody could explain why she had become bent double. Some today think that her disability had psychological causes. . . . Maybe somebody had persistently abused her, verbally or physically, when she was smaller, until her twisted-up emotions communicated themselves to her body."[1] Many think "spirit of weakness" means that she was weighed down by great griefs and burdens—possibly resentment or guilt. It doesn't appear the way demon-possession usually appears in the Gospels, though Jesus does mention Satan's involvement later (verse 16).

freed, be loosed (verses 12, 16) The Greek words, *apolyō, lyō*, mean to free fully, to relieve, release, dismiss, pardon (Strong's 630, 3089).

of Jesus' life. By this time he had explained himself many times on the issue of healing on the Sabbath. And he had many adversaries by this time.

2. *Character focus: The disabled woman.* Before reading the passage again, take a break and walk around the room bent over at the waist. Notice

what you can and can't see. Imagine for a moment that you are trying to talk to someone and notice how you have to contort yourself to do so. Notice how your head and back feel after a few minutes. How might living in this condition have affected her mental and emotional state?

Jesus called her forward, which means she didn't ask for help. What are some possible reasons she didn't ask for help?

- She thought: *Jesus can't help me*, or *Jesus wouldn't want to help me.*

- She thought: *After all, my problem is not life-threatening.*

- She thought: *Maybe God wants me bent over because of a sin I committed, and this will teach me a lesson!*

- She was afraid because of the "adversaries" who were present (verse 17).

- Other:_____

3. The world would have looked very different when the woman stood up. She would have seen the face of the one who healed her from her weakness.

   What might it have been like for her to stand up and gaze at Jesus' face that first time? Did she open her eyes enormously wide? Perhaps she stopped breathing. Perhaps she cried.

   What might this moment have been like for Jesus when he saw her stand upright and be "set free"?

4. *Character focus: Synagogue ruler.* Although he was indignant because of what Jesus did (verse 14), he didn't address Jesus directly. Instead he tried to sidestep a power struggle with Jesus and scolded the people instead.

   Jesus may have been irritated at the synagogue ruler and the adversaries, but other possibilities are more likely.

   - He may have been grieved, as he had been when the officials cared more about their Sabbath rules than healing the man with the shriveled arm (Mark 3:1-6).

- He was able to "speak the truth in love" when indirectly attacked (Ephesians 4:15).

- He may have laughed, as if to say, "Look, I know that you are merciful people! I know you are because you take care of your donkeys. So why should this woman suffer longer than a donkey? Why the double standard? Healing is the perfect thing to happen on Sabbath! What better day to relieve suffering?"

- Other:_____

5. Why do you think "the people rejoiced" at Jesus' answer?

- They knew that the healing glorified God and they were delighted with the beauty of that truth.

- They were tired of religious leaders who didn't seem to sincerely care about them.

- Other:_____

Reflect on the invitation. As you read the passage again, position yourself as a fly on the wall. What do you see, hear, taste, touch or smell? You may find yourself identifying with a particular person. If so, consider how this person would probably have felt.

- the woman who had been bent over

- someone in the synagogue who knew her and cared for her

- someone in the synagogue who knew her and despised her

- the synagogue leader

As you picture the passage, what moment, action or phrase stands out to you?

- As you watch the action unfold, what do you see? What does this cause you to think and feel?

- Why might God have caused that moment, word or phrase to stand out to you?

Reflect a little further.

- How does this passage connect with your life?

- Is there some idea, feeling or intention you need to embrace from it? If so, what is it?

- What might God be inviting you to be, know, understand, feel or even do?

Be open to the quiet and don't feel pressured to come up with an answer.

RESPOND (*ORATIO*)

Take a few minutes to respond to God about this. What do you most want to say to God about this experience in Scripture? You may want to speak to God about burdens that are obvious or buried, physical or mental.

You may wish to ask God questions (the answers to which may come to you later). You may wish to write out your prayer. Sometimes that helps keep our minds from wandering.

REST (*CONTEMPLATIO*)

Soak in the picture of Jesus interacting with the woman. What is most significant to you about Jesus? How does Jesus seem to you? What does this tell you about what God is like?

Spend a few minutes resting in the thoughts that have come to you. This may take the form of worship or simply resting in God's presence.

TRYING IT ON (*INCARNATIO*)

Spend some time in quiet and ask God if you have deeper hurts that God wishes to heal. If you sense this is so, ask God what might be your next step. If there is someone you trust to speak to about this, ask God to help you arrange this.

27

Knowing That God Hears Me

Mark 5:24-34

RELAX AND REFOCUS (*SILENCIO*)

Inhale and exhale a few times. Let go of distractions. Quiet your thoughts and open yourself to God.

Optional—If you need to focus a little more, you might ask yourself to consider the last time you felt truly heard by someone.

READ (*LECTIO*)

Read the passage to yourself. Then read the notes below it about the key words and phrases. Consider how these details affect your understanding of the story. Then read the passage aloud slowly. Take time to let the words "fall on your ear."

REFLECT (*MEDITATIO*)

Questions and cues to help you enter into the story.

1. *Cultural background: Wholeness for the Jews.*

- *Legality*: When someone was healed they went to the priests, who were the health inspectors. The priests certified the healing and declared the person clean. Being healed in public eased that process, since there would be witnesses to the healing.

Mark 5:24–34

24So Jesus went with *him*.

A large crowd followed and pressed around him. **25**And a woman was there who had been *subject to bleeding for twelve years*. **26**She had suffered a great deal under the care of many doctors and had spent all she had, yet instead of getting better she grew worse. **27**When she heard about Jesus, she came up behind him in the crowd and touched his cloak, **28**because she thought, "If I just *touch his clothes*, I will be healed." **29**Immediately her bleeding stopped and she felt in her body that she was freed from her suffering.

30At once Jesus realized that power had gone out from him. He turned around in the crowd and asked, "*Who touched my clothes?*"

31"You see the people crowding against you," his disciples answered, "and yet you can ask, 'Who touched me?'"

32But Jesus kept looking around to see who had done it. **33**Then the woman, knowing what had happened to her, came and fell at his feet and, trembling with fear, told him the whole truth. **34**He said to her, "Daughter, your faith has healed you. Go in peace and be freed from your suffering."

---

him This pronoun refers to Jairus, the synagogue ruler who had begged Jesus to come and heal his daughter, who was dying.
subject to bleeding for twelve years This bleeding would have made the woman ritually unclean (Leviticus 15:25-27) and excluded her from social contact with others, including attendance at the synagogue.
touch his clothes Skin contact with Jesus would have made him ceremonially unclean. She may have thought that by touching his clothes she wasn't putting him at risk, or that even if she did, at least he wouldn't know it.
Who touched my clothes? Jesus may not have known who did it, or he may have known but wanted to meet her face to face. He knew it was important that she present herself to him.

- *Public interaction*: The woman would have been shunned for all these years. She would not have been able to go to the synagogue or the market. She would not have been able to embrace her family.

- *Societal restoration*: After her healing, she was not only free to mix in public, but she would have been a local celebrity because Jesus complimented her faith publicly: "Daughter, your faith has healed you" (verse 34). The crowd would have noticed that Jesus used the term "Daughter," which was a term of endearment.

2. This woman had many reasons to be desperate:

- She had visited many doctors. The Talmud gives eleven cures for continuous hemorrhaging—tonics, astringents and even superstitions, such as carrying an ostrich egg in a linen rag in the summer and in a cotton rag in winter.[1]

- She had spent all she had.

- She had gotten worse instead of better.

When have you felt desperate? Did it lead you to do something extraordinary? If so, what?

3. *Fly on the wall cue: Picture the woman telling the whole truth.* It would have taken some time for the woman to tell Jesus "the whole truth" (verse 33), which may have included that she had been the one who touched his clothes. She may also have told Jesus

- why she touched his clothes instead of talking directly to him (that she had kept him from becoming "unclean" through contact with her);

- her medical history (how many doctors she'd seen, how much money she'd spent);

- her feelings of being looked down upon as unclean and unable to join in worship; and

- the social and psychological effects of having been unclean for twelve years.

Perhaps the woman had debated within herself whether she should approach Jesus. Here are a few possible arguments for and against:

AGAINST APPROACHING JESUS	FOR APPROACHING JESUS
Timidity (What if she got caught? What if someone recognized her?)	Superstitious thinking that his clothes might be wired with power
Embarrassment at speaking about such an ailment in a public crowd	Sneaking up behind him and touching his clothes might not be detected
Concern that Jesus would have become unclean by interacting with her	Not touching her but her touching his clothes would be all right
He was in a hurry to help Jairus's daughter	She could touch his clothes without delaying him
Other:	Other:

4. You might picture the woman falling at Jesus' feet (verse 33) but it's likely that by the time she told her story, they had significant eye contact as she spoke. Perhaps it happened this way:

> From the moment Jesus was face to face with the woman, there seems to be nobody there but He and she. It happened in the middle of the crowd; but the crowd was forgotten and Jesus spoke to that woman and treated her as if she was the only person in the world.[2]

If you wish, put yourself in the woman's place. Close your eyes and see yourself standing or sitting face to face with Jesus. He is listening to you tell your "whole truth." It's as if there's nobody there but you and him. This picture in your mind reflects the reality of God attentively listening to our prayers (Psalm 65:2; 66:19; 102:17; 145:18, 19). Reflect on this in silence for a few minutes.

5. Based on all of the above information, what sort of facial expression do you think Jesus had as he listened to her?

6. *Cultural background: The cloak.* Men wore an inner garment close to their skin and an outer garment wrapped at the waist with a wide cloth or leather belt, called a girdle. According to Jewish law, this outer garment was supposed to have two fringes hung at the bottom and

two hung over the shoulders where the cloak folded over (Numbers 15:37-40; Deuteronomy 22:12). The woman probably touched the fringe of Jesus' cloak. In addition, great teachers whom the Jews considered rabbis (Jesus was called *rabbi*—see John 1:49; 6:25) also wore a *tallit*—a rectangular or square outer garment worn over the top of the body. This had a tassel or fringe at each of its four corners.[3]

Reflect on the invitation. Read the passage aloud again. Picture what the scene would look like. Hear the words clearly. Feel the pressure of a noisy, teeming crowd. Their nostrils were full of the smell of sweat.

- As you picture the passage, what moment, action or phrase stands out to you?

- As you watch the action unfold, what do you see? What does this cause you to think and feel?

- Why might God have caused that moment, word or phrase to stand out to you?

Reflect a little further.

- How does this passage connect with your life?

- Is there some idea, feeling or intention you need to embrace from it? If so, what?

- What might God be inviting you to be or know or understand about yourself or someone else?

RESPOND (*ORATIO*)

Take a few minutes to respond to God about this. You may wish to tell God your "whole truth" about something, remembering that God listens attentively when we speak.

REST (*CONTEMPLATIO*)

Soak in the picture of Jesus interacting with the crowd and then the woman. What is most significant to you about Jesus? How does Jesus seem to you?

Spend a few minutes resting in the thoughts that have come to you. This may take the form of worship or simply resting in God's presence.

Trying It On (*INCARNATIO*)

Look for someone in your life who needs to be heard. In the moment when you sense this, ask God to give you a sense of presence that pays careful attention to that person. Consider this is exactly what Jesus was like.

28

Are You Willing
to Be Healed?

John 5:1-9

RELAX AND REFOCUS (*SILENCIO*)

Inhale and exhale a few times. Let go of distractions. Quiet your thoughts
and open yourself to God.

Optional—Ask yourself the following question to help focus your
thoughts for meditation on today's passage. What does it feel like when
your life is at a standstill?

READ (*LECTIO*)

Read the passage to yourself. Then read the notes below it about the key
words and phrases. Consider how these details affect your understanding
of the story. Then read the passage aloud slowly. Take time to let the
words "fall on your ear."

REFLECT (*MEDITATIO*)

Questions and cues to help you enter into the story.

1. *Fly on the wall cue: Picture the Pool of Bethesda.* This healing took place
   at a sheep gate in Jerusalem's huge city wall, next to a pool with five
   porches. Historians can't identify this structure for certain, so we don't

John 5:1-9

¹Some time later, Jesus went up to Jerusalem for one of the Jewish festivals. ²Now there is in Jerusalem near the Sheep Gate a pool, which in Aramaic is called Bethesda and which is surrounded by five covered colonnades. ³Here a **great number of disabled people** used to lie—the blind, the lame, the paralyzed. [4] ⁵One who was there had been an invalid for thirty-eight years.

⁶When Jesus saw him lying there and learned that he had been in this condition for a long time, he asked him, "Do you want to get well?"

⁷"Sir," the invalid replied, "I have no one to help me into the pool when the water is stirred. While I am trying to get in, someone else goes down ahead of me."

⁸Then Jesus said to him, "Get up! Pick up your mat and walk." ⁹At once the man was **cured**; he picked up his mat and walked.

---

great number of disabled people Jesus may have healed many or all of these people, but John has chosen to focus on this man because of the heat his healing generated later among the Pharisees (John 5:10-15).
cured This cure was complex. Not only was the man's physical disability cured, but also thirty-eight years of muscle deterioration. What's more, people often can't stand upright without fainting after not standing for just a few weeks. But this man stood and walked—apparently without limping, fainting or falling.

know what it looked like. It may have been a gazebo-type structure with a pentagon-shaped border and a pool in the middle. In Jerusalem today there are mineral springs on the east side of the city, and the pool may have been fed by one of them.[1] This might explain the stirring of the water and its reputation for curing. The bed the disabled man picked up was probably a mat of woven fabric or cloth.

2. *Context: Jesus as initiator of healing.* Most of the time Jesus healed people who asked for help, or when someone who loved a person asked for help. But in about a third of the healings recorded in

the Gospels, Jesus himself initiated the healing. Often this was in a synagogue, such as the man with the shriveled arm and the woman who was bent over (Mark 3:1-6; Luke 13:10-17). This healing is unusual in that Jesus approached the disabled man in a public place.

In addition, Jesus asked the man, "Do you want to get well?" even though the man had already stationed himself in a place where healings were supposed to occur.

Why might Jesus have asked this question?

- Jesus was asking the man because the man didn't ask him.

- The man had lost hope and was afraid to ask in case the healing didn't work.

- The man didn't ask Jesus for help because he doubted Jesus' power or goodness.

- The man had given up on getting well.

- Getting well may have frightened him, since it would mean he'd have to support himself and have normal relationships.

- Other:_____

3. *Willingness.* If the man had given up on getting well, he may have felt trapped and helpless. When, if ever, have you gotten so used to a bad situation that you stopped trying to resolve it?

4. Consider the man's reply: "I have no one to help me" (verse 7). Can you remember a time when there was no one to help you and you could not move forward? Perhaps you lacked the resources you needed. List a few areas in your life that are at a standstill.

1.

2.

3.

Reflect on the invitation. Read the passage aloud again. Picture what the scene would look like. This seems to have been a crowded place. Hear Jesus and the man speak. Picture the man carefully trying to stand up and finding himself able to do so. What might have been the look on his face?

- As you picture the passage, what moment, action or phrase stands out to you?

- As you watch the action unfold, what do you see? What does this cause you to think and feel?

- Why might God have caused that moment, word or phrase to stand out to you?

Reflect a little further.

- How does this passage connect with your life?

- Is there some idea, feeling or intention you need to embrace from it? If so, what is it?

- What might God be inviting you to be, know, understand, feel or even do?

Be open to the quiet and don't feel pressured to come up with an answer.

Respond (*ORATIO*)

Take a few minutes to respond to God about this. Is there something you need to risk? Is there an area of life where you want to be made well? What do you most want to say to God about this experience in Scripture?

Rest (*CONTEMPLATIO*)

Soak in the picture of Jesus interacting with the man. What is most significant to you about Jesus? How does Jesus seem to you? What does this tell you about what God is like?

Spend a few minutes resting in the thoughts that have come to you. This may take the form of worship or simply resting in God's presence.

TRYING IT ON (*INCARNATIO*)

Be open to God inviting you to risk something in a situation you thought was closed or helpless. Maybe God wants to heal you there. Maybe God wants to move you forward out of your predicament.

Ask God what you need to know or do about that.

Writing Your Prayers

*The third phase of lectio divina is **oratio**, which means "prayer" in Latin. The English word used for this phase is "respond." When someone speaks to us, it's courteous to respond. So we also respond to what God has said to us. This is not automatic. Sometimes we search the Bible for nuggets, feel satisfied when we find them and then move on without responding to God. Thus we miss a greater engagement with God in Scripture.*

Responding to God is crucial. The four-phase lectio process insists that we digest the Word. It invites us to into a conversation with God.

*During the **oratio** phase, consider: What do you most want to say to God about your experience in Scripture? What stood out to you? Did it disturb you or delight you? Do you need to ask God for the next step?*

Writing your response down in words forces you to think more clearly and concretely. Holding a pen anchors you. If it helps you to use colored pens to write with or sketch out how the scene looks to you, please do so. This concrete response will cause deeper thoughts and feelings to emerge. You may be surprised by how deeply you respond.

If you're afraid someone will find what you write, you can tear it up when you're done. Or you can compose your prayer on your computer and then erase it. Do whatever it takes to enter into an honest response to God.

29

Moving from Mourning to Dancing

Psalm 30

RELAX AND REFOCUS (*SILENCIO*)

Center yourself by breathing in and out. Relax your neck and breathe out again. Let your shoulders relax.

Optional—Consider the "pits" God has pulled you out of in the past.

READ (*LECTIO*)

Read the passage to yourself silently. Then read the notes below it about the key words and phrases. Consider how these details help your understanding of the passage. Then read the passage aloud slowly. Take time to let the words "fall on your ear."

REFLECT (*MEDITATIO*)

Questions and cues to help you reflect on the passage.

1. *Character focus: God and momentary anger.* Psalm 103 describes God as "slow to anger." God doesn't fly off the handle. Instead, God is extraordinarily patient. "He will not always accuse, nor will he harbor his anger forever" (Psalm 103:9). God doesn't sulk or hold grudges. Consider that:

Psalm 30 (NCV)

A psalm of David. A song for giving the Temple to the Lord.

¹I will praise you, LORD,
    because you rescued me.
    You did not let my enemies laugh at me.
²LORD, my God, I prayed to you,
    and you healed me.
³You lifted me out of the grave;
    you spared me from going down to the place of the dead.
⁴Sing praises to the LORD, you who belong to him;
    praise his holy name.
⁵His **anger lasts only a moment**,
    but his kindness lasts for a lifetime.
Crying may last for a night,
    but joy comes in the morning.
⁶When I felt safe, I said,
    "I will never fear."
⁷LORD, in your kindness you made my mountain safe.
    But when you turned away, I was frightened.
⁸I called to you, LORD,
    and asked you to have mercy on me.
⁹I said, "What good will it do if I die
    or if I go down to the grave?
Dust cannot praise you;
    it cannot speak about your truth.
¹⁰LORD, hear me and have mercy on me.
    LORD, help me."

---

anger lasts only a moment God's anger is not capricious, bad tempered or given to fits, but a dimension of divine justice and fairness. Like the sting of a flu shot or the temporary discomfort of an operation, God's anger—justice—does its work quickly.

> [11]You changed my sorrow into danging.
>   You took away my *clothes of sadness*,
>   and clothed me in happiness.
> [12]I will sing to you and not be silent.
>   LORD, my God, I will praise you forever.
>
> ---
>
> *clothes of sadness* In mourning, people in the psalmist's time would have worn
> itchy, coarse material around their waist next to their skin. They often tore their
> clothes to demonstrate their grief.

God's anger is not like man's anger. People often view God as a
projection of their own personality. If, when you get mad, you want
to punch people, you may assume God wants the same. If you sulk
and turn anger inward, you may act as if God smolders at you.
God's anger is different from man's anger: "Because I am God,
and not man—the Holy One among you—I will not come in
wrath" (Hosea 11:9 NET). God gets angry in response to human
moral lapses, but He does not have temper tantrums. Unlike us,
He manages to be fair even when He's angry. God delights in
showing mercy, not in showing off His power in irrational,
thoughtless actions (Micah 7:18).[1]

In Psalms 86, 103 and 145, "slow to anger" is paired with "abounding
in steadfast love" (NRSV).

Why is it important to understand the nature of God's anger?

2. *Contemporary comparison: "Enemies" (verse 1)*. Enemies take many
forms in your life. Sometimes they are

- someone you find difficult, and so avoid

- someone you just can't seem to love

- someone who seems to oppose everything you do

- someone who has betrayed you in the past

- yourself, when you dwell on activities that are not God's will for you
- yourself, when your thoughts spin into negative spirals
- Other:_____

3. *Contemporary comparison: "Grave" and "place of the dead" (verse 3).* What have been your "pits" in life?

- rejection by someone (_____)
- depression
- a time when you were forced to leave a job
- loneliness
- financial struggles
- health struggles
- failure
- Other:_____

4. *Contemporary comparison: Dancing (verse 11).* How might joyful dancing translate in your life?

- dancing with someone
- doing a few dance steps where no one else can see you
- raising your arms and shouting at a favorite hiking spot
- running in a beautiful place, such as the beach
- listening to your favorite music and singing along
- doing a workout exercise that feels like dancing
- Other:_____

5. *Contemporary comparison: Gritty praying.* Verses 2 and 3 indicate the psalmist prayed in his worst moment. How easy is it for you to pray honest prayers when you are in your worst moments—especially when that worst moment is your fault?

- difficult because praying is the last thing I think about doing
- difficult because I can't be that honest with God
- easier than it used to be
- almost a first impulse
- Other:_____

Reflect on the invitation. Perhaps God is offering you an invitation in this passage to enlarge your understanding about something. What might that be? Read the passage again and then sit quietly for a few minutes, pondering these questions:

- What word or phrase stands out to you?
- Why do you think that is?

Reflect a little further. You may wish to read the passage again. Then consider:

- How does this passage connect with your life?
- Is there some idea, feeling or intention you need to embrace from it? If so, what is it?
- What might God be inviting you to be, know, understand, feel or even do?

Be open to the quiet and don't feel pressured to come up with an answer.

RESPOND (*ORATIO*)

Take a few minutes to respond to what you have heard from God. Say what you most wish to say to God about this experience in Scripture.

REST (*CONTEMPLATIO*)

Soak in what has stood out to you in this passage and consider: When you think of how God rescues us (even from ourselves), what feeling do you experience? Rest in that feeling.

Spend a few minutes resting in the thoughts that have come to you. This may take the form of worship (using verses 1, 4, 11 and 12) or simply resting in God's presence.

TRYING IT ON (*INCARNATIO*)

Recall with God one or two times where God has rescued you from a difficult situation. If possible, find a way to "dance" about it!

30

Receiving Jesus' Words to Caregivers

Mark 9:14-29

RELAX AND REFOCUS (*SILENCIO*)

Center yourself by breathing in and out. Relax your neck and breathe out again. Let your shoulders relax.

Optional—Ponder this question. Have you ever been a caregiver before (to a child, a younger sibling, an aging relative, an injured or sick spouse)? If so, what was that experience like? Check as many boxes as are appropriate.

☐ I sensed God's comfort at times.

☐ It was draining.

☐ It encroached on my life.

☐ It made me cry at times.

☐ It felt like God's work at times.

☐ Other: _____

READ (*LECTIO*)

Read the passage to yourself. Then read the notes below it about the key words and phrases. Consider how these details affect your understanding of the story. Then read the passage aloud slowly. Take time to let the words "fall on your ear."

Mark 9:14–29

14When **they** came to the other disciples, they saw a large crowd around them and the **teachers of the law** arguing with them. **15**As soon as all the people saw Jesus, they were overwhelmed with wonder and ran to greet him.

16"What are you arguing with them about?" he asked.

17A man in the crowd answered, "Teacher, I brought you my son, who is **possessed by a spirit** that has robbed him of speech. **18**Whenever it seizes him, it throws him to the ground. He foams at the mouth, gnashes his teeth and becomes rigid. I asked your disciples to drive out the spirit, but they could not."

19"You **unbelieving generation**," Jesus replied, "how long shall I stay with you? How long shall I **put up with you**? Bring the boy to me."

20So they brought him. When the spirit saw Jesus, it immediately threw the boy into a convulsion. He fell to the ground and rolled around, foaming at the mouth.

21Jesus asked the boy's father, "How long has he been like this?"

"From childhood," he answered. **22**"It has often thrown him into fire or water to kill him. But if you can do anything, take pity on us and help us."

23"'If you can'?" said Jesus. "Everything is possible for one who believes."

24Immediately the boy's father exclaimed, "I do believe; help me overcome my unbelief!"

---

they Jesus, Peter, James and John, who were just returning from the place of Jesus' transfiguration.

teachers of the law These scribes had tried to discredit Jesus, and now they had his disciples arguing and unable to show Jesus' authority and power as the Son of God.

possessed by a spirit A spirit from the enemy controlled this boy's actions, giving him symptoms similar to epilepsy.

unbelieving generation Jesus may have been addressing his disciples, who had cast out demons successfully in the past (Mark 6:13) and who struggled with hardness of heart (Mark 6:52; 8:17), or the teachers of the law, who also showed hardness of heart (Mark 3:5-6), or the Jews in general (Matthew 13:15; Mark 10:5; John 12:40).

put up with you The Greek word, *anechomai* (Strong's 430), means "to bear with," which is the same word Paul used when he told the Colossians to "bear with" one another (Colossians 3:13). Paul was urging them to be willingly patient with each other. This is different from our idea of "putting up" with others, when we might roll our eyes in an exasperated way.

> **25**When Jesus saw that a crowd was running to the scene, he rebuked the evil spirit. "You deaf and mute spirit," he said, "I command you, come out of him and never enter him again."
>
> **26**The spirit shrieked, convulsed him violently and came out. The boy looked so much like a corpse that many said, "He's dead." **27**But Jesus took him by the hand and lifted him to his feet, and he stood up.
>
> **28**After Jesus had gone indoors, his disciples asked him privately, "Why couldn't we drive it out?"
>
> **29**He replied, "This kind can come out only by prayer."

REFLECT (*MEDITATIO*)

Questions and cues to help you enter into the story.

1. *Context: The father as a caregiver.* The father's role in the boy's life seems to have been central. No other parent is mentioned. The mother may or may not have been alive, but certainly such a boy would have needed several caregivers. We are told that the boy had *often* been thrown into the fire and water by the demon. No doubt the father was one of the people who had rescued him. The son's plight so affects the father that he says to Jesus, "Take pity on *us* and help *us*."

2. How does Jesus respond to the father's admission of his doubts?

   • "If you can do anything, take pity on us and help us" (verse 22).

   • "I do believe; help me overcome my unbelief!" (verse 24).

3. The father expressed both doubt and belief (verse 24). Are there things about which you have both faith and doubt—the tenants of the faith, crises in the world, your family, your health, your church?

4. *Cultural background: The teachers of the law.* The teachers of the law (or scribes) were not necessarily Pharisees, although these two groups generally appeared together. Teachers of the law were judges in

religious tribunals. They had social status and held an office. They were generally regarded as the mouthpiece and representative of the people, posing questions, urging objections, expecting explanations and respectful behaviors.[1]

5. *Fly on the wall cue: Picture the boy's condition.* The young boy

- was dirty and disheveled, with foam coming out of his mouth (verse 20);

- might have had burn marks on his body from when the demon had thrown him into fires (verse 22);

- might have had marks of battering from convulsions (verses 20, 22); and

- was probably startled by the noise of the crowd and by his own voice after so many years of being deaf and mute (verse 25).

6. *Fly on the wall cue: Picture the remoteness of the location.* About this time, Jesus was traveling around the Sea of Galilee, in and out of Jewish territory. He was far from the Jewish capital (Jerusalem), but the teachers of the law were present anyway. This indicates their keen interest in Jesus, of which he was well aware.

Before reading the passage again, consider which of the following viewpoints to take. You can choose more than one if you wish.

- *The teachers of the law.* Your primary interest is orthodoxy, and you're concerned about this upstart preacher, Jesus, who doesn't do things in the conventional way of the Pharisees.

- *The disciples.* Your primary interest is casting out a demon, which you have seen Jesus do many times. You may even be frustrated—after all, Jesus commanded you to drive out demons (Matthew 10:8) and he gave you authority to do so (Mark 3:15).

- *The father of the demon-possessed boy.* You want your son healed. You have endured the demon's torture of him for a long time.

- *The boy.* You have lived a silent life, at least since childhood. Your soul has been dominated and tortured by a demon. You have been battered and burned. Other people talk to each other, but you have no part in this.

Reflect on the invitation. Read the passage aloud again. Picture what the scene would look like. Hear the words clearly.

- As you picture the passage, what moment, action or phrase stands out to you? What does this cause you to think and feel?

- Why might God have caused that moment, word or phrase to stand out to you?

Reflect a little further.

- How does this passage connect with your life?

- Is there some idea, feeling or intention you need to embrace from it? If so, what is it?

- What might God be inviting you to know, understand, feel or do?

Be open to the quiet and don't feel pressured to come up with an answer.

RESPOND (*ORATIO*)

Take a few minutes to respond to God about anything that has come to you. What do you most need to say to God at this moment?

REST (*CONTEMPLATIO*)

Soak in the picture of Jesus interacting with people in this passage. How does Jesus seem to you? What does this tell you about what God is like? Rest in the beauty of who Jesus is.

TRYING IT ON (*INCARNATIO*)

Consider someone you know who is a caregiver. Is God leading you to care for them in any way?

31

Loving Others in Truth and Action

James 1:19-27

RELAX AND REFOCUS (*SILENCIO*)

Center yourself by breathing in and out. Relax your neck and take time to let your muscles relax.

Optional—If you need to focus, you might read this prayer of Mother Teresa of Calcutta.

> Dearest Lord, may I see you today and every day in the person of your sick, and, whilst nursing them, minister unto you.
>
> Though you hide yourself behind the unattractive disguise of the irritable, the exacting, the unreasonable, may I still recognize you, and say: "Jesus, my patient, how sweet it is to serve you."
>
> And O God, while you are Jesus my patient, deign also to be to me a patient Jesus, bearing with my faults, looking only to my intention, which is to love and serve you in the person of each one of your sick.
>
> Lord, increase my faith, bless my efforts and work, now and for evermore, Amen.[1]

READ (*LECTIO*)

Read the passage to yourself silently. Then read the notes below it about the key words and phrases. Consider how these details help your understanding of the passage. Then read the passage aloud slowly. Take time to let the words "fall on your ear."

James 1:19-27

19My dear brothers and sisters, take note of this: Everyone should be quick to listen, slow to speak and slow to become angry, **20**because human anger does not produce the **righteousness** that God desires. **21**Therefore, get rid of all moral filth and the evil that is so prevalent and humbly accept the word planted in you, which can **save** you.

22Do not merely listen to the **word**, and so deceive yourselves. Do what it says. **23**Anyone who listens to the **word** but does not do what it says is like someone who looks at his face in a mirror **24**and, after looking at himself, goes away and immediately forgets what he looks like. **25**But whoever looks intently into the perfect law that gives freedom, and continues in it—not forgetting what they have heard, but doing it—they will be blessed in what they do.

26Those who consider themselves religious and yet do not keep a tight rein on their tongues deceive themselves, and their religion is worthless. **27**Religion that God our Father accepts as pure and faultless is this: to look after orphans and widows in their distress and to keep oneself from being **polluted** by the world.

---

righteousness The Greek word, *dikaiosunē* (Strong's 1343), suggests a deep, attractive inner goodness. (See also chapter eleven in this book, "Relying on the Kingdom of God.") "The best translation of *dikaiosunē* would be a paraphrase: something like 'what that is about a person that makes him or her really right or good.' For short, we might say 'true inner goodness.'"[2]
save The Greek word, *sōzō* (Strong's 4982), means to deliver or protect, to heal, preserve, save, to do well or be made whole.
word "This presumably means both the teaching of the Old Testament and the message about Jesus."[3]
polluted The Greek word, *aspilos* (Strong's 784), means unblemished physically or morally.

REFLECT (*MEDITATIO*)

Questions and cues to help you reflect on the passage.

1. *Fly on the wall cue: Picture James.* The writer is probably the brother of Jesus, who was also the leader of the Jerusalem church (Acts 15:13; 21:18)—James the apostle had already been martyred (Acts 12:2). The Jerusalem church had been persecuted and many were needy—so needy that other churches sent offerings to help them (Romans 15:25-26). Even though they were needy, James urged them to help others (verse 27).

2. N. T. Wright translates verse 20 this way: "Human anger, you see, does not produce God's justice."[4] He goes on to comment:

   > If what we want is God's justice, coming to sort things out, we will do better to get entirely out of the way and let God do his own work, rather than supposing our burst of anger (which will most likely have all sorts of nasty bits to it, such as wounded pride, malice and envy) will somehow help God do what needs to be done.[5]

   What does human anger usually produce? What produces God's justice?

3. *The power of the implanted Word (verse 21).* Other people's anger doesn't change us but we are changed through interaction with God through God's Word implanted in us—engrafted, inserted so deep inside us that it seems to grow out of us. This embedding of God's Word happens as we "humbly accept" or even "welcome with meekness" God's ideas (verse 21, NIV and NRSV).

   Consider the person who welcomes humbly and meekly what God says. What is this person's view of God? What do they want in life? How do they *feel* about what God says to them?

4. Consider verse 22: "and so deceive yourselves." We think of listening to God's Word (taught, read or preached) as a good thing, and it is. How can it be deceptive?

5. Consider verse 25: "blessed in what they do." In what way does embracing God's ideas and words deliver, protect or heal us?

6. In verse 25 James refers to "the perfect law that gives freedom." The idea that obedience to God brings freedom might sound odd to some. How might that be true?

Reflect on the invitation. Perhaps God is offering you an invitation in this passage to enlarge your understanding about something. What might that be? Read the passage again and then sit quietly for a few minutes, pondering these questions:

- What word or phrase stands out to you?

- Why do you think that is?

Reflect a little further. You may wish to read the passage again. Then consider:

- How does this passage connect with your life?

- Is there some idea, feeling or intention you need to embrace from it? If so, what is it?

- What might God be inviting you to be, know, understand, feel or even do?

Be open to the quiet and don't feel pressured to come up with an answer.

Respond (*ORATIO*)

Take a few minutes to respond to what you have heard from God. Say what you most wish to say to God about this experience in Scripture?

If you have questions about the passage, you might ask God about this, the answers to which may come to you through the group or later in the week. (For example: How does obedience bring freedom?) You may wish to write your prayer down. Sometimes that helps to keep our minds from wandering.

Rest (*CONTEMPLATIO*)

This passage demands a high level of active obedience. Yet it all flows from embracing the Word of God and the wholeness and freedom that comes from that. Try to rest in the idea that God equips us to obey and empowers us to obey.

Spend a few minutes noticing the thoughts that have come to you. This may take the form of worship or simply resting in God's presence.

Trying It On (*INCARNATIO*)

Ask God to help you *do* something mentioned in this passage. Be quick to listen; refuse to be impatient and angry; look after someone in need; make a decision that keeps you from being weakened by the world.

If you wish, pray the opening prayer by Mother Teresa for a specific person or situation.

Moving from Self-Absorption to Humility

Philippians 2:1-16

RELAX AND REFOCUS (*SILENCIO*)

Center yourself by breathing in and out. Relax your neck and take time to let your muscles relax.

Optional—If you need to focus, ponder this question: What color comes to mind when you think of humility? Why?

READ (*LECTIO*)

Read the passage to yourself silently. Then read the notes below it about the key words and phrases. Consider how these details help your understanding of the passage. Then read the passage aloud slowly. Take time to let the words "fall on your ear."

REFLECT (*MEDITATIO*)

Questions and cues to help you reflect on the passage.

1. *Self-giving love.* Love has many meanings in contemporary culture. The Greek word *agapē*, used here, refers to self-giving love: self-sacrificing and unselfish behavior, willingness to deprive oneself and to give voluntarily without expecting compensation.

Philippians 2:1-16

¹Therefore if you have any encouragement from being united with Christ, if any comfort from his love, if any common sharing in the Spirit, if any tenderness and compassion, ²then make my joy complete by being like-minded, having the same love, being one in spirit and of one mind. ³Do nothing out of selfish ambition or ***vain*** conceit. Rather, in ***humility*** value others above yourselves, ⁴not looking to your own interests but each of you to the interests of the others.

⁵In your relationships with one another, have the same mindset as Christ Jesus:

⁶Who, being in very nature God,
    did not consider equality with God something to be used to his own
        advantage;
⁷rather, he made himself nothing
    by taking the very nature of a servant,
    being made in human likeness.
⁸And being found in appearance as a man,
    he humbled himself
by becoming obedient to death—
    even death on a cross!

⁹Therefore God exalted him to the highest place
    and gave him the name that is above every name,
¹⁰that at the name of Jesus every knee should bow,
    in heaven and on earth and under the earth,
¹¹and every tongue acknowledge that Jesus Christ is Lord,
    to the glory of God the Father.

vain Egotistical or empty, self-glorifying; pushing your way to the front (Philippians 2:3 *The Message*).
humility Not pushing ahead; preoccupation with God rather than with self.

¹²Therefore, my dear friends, as you have always obeyed—not only in my presence, but now much more in my absence—continue to work out your salvation with fear and trembling, ¹³for it is God who works in you to will and to act in order to fulfill his good purpose.

¹⁴Do everything without grumbling or arguing, ¹⁵so that you may become blameless and *pure*, "children of God without fault in a warped and crooked generation." Then you will shine among them like stars in the sky ¹⁶as you hold firmly to the word of life. And then I will be able to *boast* on the day of Christ that I did not run or labor in vain.

pure Harmless, sincere; used to describe wine unmixed with water or unalloyed metal. Without mixed motives—a breath of fresh air in a polluted society (Philippians 2:15 *The Message*).
boast Brag, but in the sense of rejoicing; Paul would be proud of the Philippians.

When have you seen someone exhibit self-giving love? What did you think of it?

2. *Union with God.* This passage begins with four if-then clauses (verse 1). Paul's point seems to have been, "If you're experiencing union with God, then do what it takes to unite yourself with others." The beauty of this is that God isn't just telling us to try harder to be humble or to love people, but to take the overflow of love and grace we've received from God and give it to others.

Paul described experiencing union with God in these ways:

☐ being encouraged by this union

☐ finding comfort in God's love

☐ fellowshipping with the Spirit

☐ experiencing the tenderness and compassion of God

Reread these phrases and then sit and look at them for a minute or two. Then check the ones you've experienced within the last few months.

3. *Union with each other.* Paul described the unity we have with each other in these ways:

- loyalty toward each other even when we don't agree
- loving each other with the self-sacrificing love of Christ
- harmony of feeling
- having common purposes and goals[1]

When have you experienced such unity with others "in Christ"?

4. *Working against self-absorption.* The phrase "value others above yourselves" is not suggesting we have low self-worth, but that we not be self-absorbed (verse 3). Instead of being preoccupied with ourselves, we are preoccupied with God and with how God is inviting us to love others. That is the core of humility. To imitate Christ, who "did not consider equality with God something to be used to his own advantage," means we don't look for ways to win in every situation or for ways to make things work for us (verse 6). It urges us to ask, Do I give most of my thoughts and time to meeting my own needs? Is everything about me? It's human nature to be self-obsessed, but God invites us to imitate Christ and let go of being self-focused.

Consider what we might say to God when we find ourselves absorbed in selfish ambition and personal prestige, trying to impress people or be sought after.

- What does this other person need?
- Help me see that everything isn't about me.
- Help me to focus on you, God, and what you are doing today in this world.
- Other:_____

5. *Trusting God throughout.* "Do everything without complaining or arguing" (verse 14) doesn't mean that we shouldn't ask questions or

make suggestions, but that we can trust God and keep a right heart (Proverbs 4:23). Do I have a reconciler's heart or a complainer's heart? To have a reconciler's heart may mean that before I complain or disagree with someone, I

- consider where others are coming from (their apparent emotions and motives);
- pray for the other people involved;
- try to get to know the other people involved; or
- ask myself if I have any reason to hold a grudge against these people or this cause.
- Other:_____

6. *Fly on the wall cue: Picture the Philippian church.* The Philippian church would have included diverse people (Acts 16:12-40), who might have found unity difficult. For example, there was

- a prison jailer (a middle-class civil servant), who when he thought his prisoners had escaped would have killed himself if Paul had not stopped him;
- a rich fabric merchant, Lydia, with whom Paul and Silas stayed (Acts 16:11-15); and
- a demon-possessed slave girl who told fortunes (Acts 16:16-18).

Put yourself in the place of someone who is part of the Philippian church. Who would have been most difficult for you to "value above yourself"?

7. *Fly on the wall cue: Picture the city, Philippi.* Philippi was a Roman colony and the leading city of the district of Macedonia. It was focused on getting ahead.[2] Paul's words about humility and unity would have been radical. When Paul and Silas first came there, they preached outside the city gate by the river and the church may have continued to meet beyond the watchful eyes of officials.

Read this passage again—aloud, this time—and close your eyes, picturing this letter being read to the Philippian church as they sit by the river with its outdoor sounds and scents.

Reflect on the invitation. Perhaps God is offering you an invitation in this passage to enlarge your understanding about something. What might that be? Read the passage again and ponder these questions:

- What word or phrase stands out to you? Why do you think that is?

Reflect a little further. You may wish to read the passage again. Then consider:

- How does this passage connect with your life?
- Is there some idea, feeling or intention you need to embrace from it? If so, what is it?
- What might God be inviting you to know, understand, feel or do?

Be open to the quiet and don't feel pressured to come up with an answer.

Respond (*ORATIO*)

Take a few minutes to respond to what you have heard from God, especially about Christ's humble, self-giving love.

Rest (*CONTEMPLATIO*)

Soak in what has stood out to you in this passage and notice how Jesus' actions and motives seemed to you. How have you been encouraged by Christ, have a sense of unity with Christ, comfort from his love, sharing in the Spirit, and his tenderness and compassion?

Let these thoughts help you worship God or simply rest in God's presence.

Trying It On (*INCARNATIO*)

Ask God how you might taste God's self-giving love and implement it in humility. What might that look like for you?

Meditation Leads to Transformation

Perhaps there are some ways you would like to change—attitudes you need to let go of, habits you need to replace, character qualities that need to take shape. God's plan is for us to be transformed by the renewing of our minds (Romans 12:2). As we encounter God through the living, productive, penetrating Word of God, that encounter changes our minds, hearts, and even our imaginations so that we taste and see that the Lord is good (Psalm 34:8).

This meditative, interactive process directly affects behavior: "Do not let this Book of the Law depart from your mouth; meditate on it day and night, so that you may be careful to do everything written in it" (Joshua 1:8). Being "careful to do" what God says flows organically from Scripture meditation. We find ourselves putting into action what we've seen Jesus do in our imaginations. One day we are fascinated by how Jesus notices overlooked and marginalized, and the next day we find ourselves doing the same thing. Hearts of stone gradually become hearts of flesh (Ezekiel 11:19).

Transformation means looking at the sealed, stale rooms of our lives and offering all that we find to God for forgiveness, acceptance and healing. All along the way there are flashes of insight, moments of exquisite beauty, and experiences of reconciliation. We are the clay, being gradually shaped in the hands of the Potter. Participating fully in lectio divina shows our intention to be conscious and cooperative clay.

Transformation occurs slowly and progressively. Little by little, we let go of our old selves. The destructive thought habits in our heads turn into prayers of healing, and we more easily set aside negative thoughts and give them less control over our actions. Somehow it's easier to smile at a driver who is rude. It isn't a crisis. We have too much good going on with God to be bothered by it.

Loving the "Stranger"

Luke 10:25-37

RELAX AND REFOCUS (*SILENCIO*)

Center yourself by breathing in and out. Relax your neck and breathe out again. Let your shoulders relax.

Optional—If you need to focus, ponder this question: What is true about the kind of person who welcomes those who want nothing to do with them?

READ (*LECTIO*)

Read the passage to yourself. Then read the notes below it about the key words and phrases. Consider how these details affect your understanding of the story. Then read the passage aloud slowly. Take time to let the words "fall on your ear."

REFLECT (*MEDITATIO*)

Questions and cues to help you enter into the story.

1. *Cultural background: Samaritans.* During the exile of the southern kingdom of Judea to Babylonia, the Jews who had stayed behind in Palestine intermarried with non-Jews and inhabited the area around Samaria. "The hatred between Jews and Samaritans had gone on for

hundreds of years—and is still reflected, tragically, in the smouldering tension between Israel and Palestine today. Both sides claimed to be the true inheritors of the promises of Abraham and Moses . . . and rightful possessors of the land."[1]

2. *Cultural background: The "stranger."* The "stranger" was a non-Jewish person, or a foreigner. By implication it might also mean a guest. Today a stranger to you might be anyone who:

- is unfamiliar

- speaks another language

- has a different skin color

- wears different sorts of clothes

- lives a lifestyle unlike yours

- makes you afraid[2]

3. Who would be a "Samaritan" in relation to you? What would have to be true about someone to might make you think, *I'd never hang out with that person?*

- financial status (different from yours, either poorer or richer)

- job (examples: prison guard, sanitation worker, animal slaughterer)

- ethnicity

- having a disability

- having a disease

Who is the *last* person you'd want to see on the side of the road needing your help?

4. *Welcoming strangers.* Jesus said those who welcomed strangers were actually welcoming him (Matthew 25:35). "To welcome strangers means cultivating an invitational spirit and offering a sense of 'home' to others (John 14:23)—especially those who are often

Luke 10:25-37

25On one occasion an expert in the law stood up to **test** Jesus. "Teacher," he asked, "what must I do to inherit eternal life?"

26"What is written in the Law?" he replied. "How do you read it?"

27He answered, "'Love the Lord your God with all your heart and with all your soul and with all your strength and with all your mind'; and, 'Love your neighbor as yourself.'"

28"You have answered correctly," Jesus replied. "Do this and you will live."

29But he wanted to **justify** himself, so he asked Jesus, "And who is my neighbor?"

30In reply Jesus said: "A man was going down from Jerusalem to Jericho, when he was attacked by robbers. They stripped him of his clothes, beat him and went away, leaving him half dead. **31**A priest happened to be going down the same road, and when he saw the man, he passed by on the other side. **32**So too, a Levite, when he came to the place and saw him, passed by on the other side. **33**But a Samaritan, as he traveled, came where the man was; and when he saw him, he took pity on him. **34**He went to him and bandaged his wounds, pouring on oil and wine. Then he put the man on his own donkey, brought him to an inn and took care of him. **35**The next day he took out two **denarii** and gave them to the innkeeper. 'Look after him,' he said, 'and when I return, I will reimburse you for any extra expense you may have.'

36"Which of these three do you think was a neighbor to the man who fell into the hands of robbers?"

37The expert in the law replied, "The one who had mercy on him."

Jesus told him, "Go and do likewise."

---

test Alternate translation: put Jesus on the spot.[3]
justify The Greek word, *dikaioō* (Strong's 1342), means to be regarded as just or innocent or righteous. N. T. Wright translates it as "wanting to win a point."
denarii One denarius was one day's wage for a skilled laborer.

excluded. We pay attention to others, inviting them to be at home with us as they unfold themselves before us (as God invites us). Then we wait for them to be able to do that."[4] Hospitality is not only an activity, but also a condition of the heart and characteristic of our inner person.

5. *Jesus' version of a disciple: The good Samaritan.* Here are some qualities of the Samaritan. Check the qualities, if any, that you admire.

☐ Not self-conscious: He automatically helped as if it were no big deal. He didn't have to say, "I think I'll do a good deed." If you dropped something, he wouldn't hesitate to pick it up, hand it to you, smile and go on. He didn't have to go somewhere special to serve God like the priest and Levite did. Unlike the expert in the law who wanted to appear righteous, the Samaritan appears not to have been concerned with how the situation looked.

☐ Unselfish: The Samaritan wasn't cheap, but gave the innkeeper more than was needed. He didn't ask the innkeeper: How much are you going to chip in? He may have had to rearrange his schedule to take care of the beaten man. He was a giver, not a taker.

☐ Unhesitant: He didn't stand on the road and debate with himself about whether he should help (as many of us do): Should I? Shouldn't I? It wasn't complicated.

☐ Unafraid: He could have been attacked himself while he helped the man.

☐ Ordinary: He didn't do this because it was his duty. He was like you and me. He didn't go on to create the Jerusalem to Jericho Road Rescue Program. He just saw someone in front of him in need and helped that person.

☐ Empathetic: He saw someone in need and wasn't bothered that this man was his supposed enemy. He seemed to step out with the thought, "If that were me, I'd want help."

6. *Fly on the wall cue: Picture the ending of the story.* Jesus left the story somewhat unfinished.[5] Jesus' listeners might have tried to finish the story in their minds. Here are some possibilities:

- The injured man was horrified when he woke up and learned that a Samaritan had helped him.

- The injured man changed his outlook and thanked the Samaritan.

- A crowd waited outside the inn to confront the Samaritan for daring to touch a Jew.[6]

How do you think the expert in the law would have finished it?

Reflect on the invitation. Read the passage aloud again. Picture what the scene would have looked like. Hear the words clearly.

- As you picture the passage, what moment, action or phrase stands out to you?

- As you watch the action unfold, what do you see? What does this cause you to think and feel?

- Why might God have caused that moment, word or phrase to stand out to you?

Reflect a little further. As you do this, don't compare yourself to the Samaritan. Consider, instead, that God is powerful and—if we ask—can transform us into the kind of person who would help anyone in need.

- How does this passage connect with your life?

- Is there some idea, feeling or intention you need to embrace from it? If so, what is it?

- What might God be inviting you to be, know, understand, feel or even do?

Be open to the quiet and don't feel pressured to come up with an answer.

RESPOND (*ORATIO*)

Take a few minutes to respond to God about this. What do you most want to say to God about this experience in Scripture?

If this story has presented you with some struggles, please tell God about those struggles and be assured that God will tell you as much as you can stand to hear at this moment.

Rest (*CONTEMPLATIO*)

Soak in what has stood out to you in this passage and consider: What does the Samaritan tell us about what God is like?

Spend a few minutes noticing the thoughts that have come to you. This may take the form of worshiping God.

Trying It On (*INCARNATIO*)

What would it look like to love a person I don't really know? Might you be able to do that for just a few minutes? Keep in mind that loving someone is engaging the will in what is best for that person.[7]

34

Choosing Relationship over Judgment

Luke 6:36-38; Matthew 5:43-48

RELAX AND REFOCUS (*SILENCIO*)

Center yourself by breathing in and out. Relax your neck and take time to let your muscles relax.

Optional—This passage is about loving enemies and it can be difficult to read. You might even feel like it is so unattainable that you'd prefer to skip it. Here are some thoughts that might help:

1. Focus on how *Jesus* lived this (one of the questions will help you in this regard), not how distant it seems from your behavior. Concentrate on Jesus' words, not your own thoughts and feelings.

2. Focus on how it portrays the beauty of the kingdom of God. Here's a quote to help you:

The kingdom that Jesus preached and lived was all about a glorious, uproarious, absurd generosity. Think of the best thing you can do for the worst person, and go ahead and do it.... But are [these things] possible? Well, yes and no. Jesus' point was not to provide his followers with a new rule-book ... but to illustrate an attitude of heart, a lightness of spirit in the face of all that the world can throw at you.[1]

READ (*LECTIO*)

Read the passage to yourself silently. Then read the notes below it about the key words and phrases. Consider how these details help your understanding of the passage. Then read the passage aloud slowly. Take time to let the words "fall on your ear."

REFLECT (*MEDITATIO*)

Questions and cues to help you reflect on the passage.

1. *Contemporary comparison: Enemies.* The first hearers of these words probably heard the word "enemies" and thought of their Roman oppressors. The idea of loving them would have been appalling. You may not have a political oppressor, but you probably have difficult people in your life. Consider for a moment who those people are in your life. Write their initials here after each category.

   - someone you avoid
   - someone you find difficult to deal with
   - someone who treats you disrespectfully
   - someone who doesn't like you
   - someone who has hurt you (physically, emotionally, financially)
   - Other:_____

2. *Praying for an enemy.* These verses beg us to consider the humanity of those who have been unjust, and possibly inhumane, to us. This passage suggests one practical way to do this: pray for that person (verse 44). Here are some prayers to offer regarding enemies. Which ones might you be able to pray regarding a difficult person? If you don't feel ready to pray any of them, add a prayer that might be more possible for you.

   - God, show me the heart of this person.
   - God, show me your heart for this person.

Luke 6:36-38

36Be merciful, just as your Father is merciful.

37Do not judge, and you will not be judged. Do not condemn, and you will not be condemned. Forgive, and you will be forgiven. **38**Give, and it will be given to you. A good measure, pressed down, shaken together and running over, will be poured into your lap. For with the measure you use, it will be measured to you.

Matthew 5:43-48

43You have heard that it was said, "**Love** your neighbor and hate your enemy." **44**But I tell you, love your enemies and pray for those who persecute you, **45**that you may be children of your Father in heaven. He causes his sun to rise on the evil and the good, and sends rain on the righteous and the unrighteous. **46**If you love those who love you, what reward will you get? Are not even the tax collectors doing that? **47**And if you greet only your own people, what are you doing more than others? Do not even pagans do that? **48**Be **perfect**, therefore, as your heavenly Father is perfect.

love Engaging the will for the good of another person. It involves respecting someone, being kind to them and meeting their needs as you are able. This doesn't require affection, but it does help to have a heart for that person.[2]

perfect The Greek word, *teleios* (Strong's 5056), is the same word Jesus used on the cross when he said, "It is finished." It means "complete" (in various applications of labor, growth, mental and moral character). It implies completion and maturity. Love completes the law, which is why Jesus said that the Law and the prophets hang on these two commandments: to love God and love your neighbor (Matthew 22:37-40).

- What does this person need from me?
- What does this person need from you?

- Is there anything I can do to reconcile with this person?
- God, give me your heart of love and compassion for this person.
- Other:_____

3. *Looking at Jesus.* Let's shift the emphasis to the behavior of Jesus and how Jesus showed love to his enemies. Read the examples in the table. Which of these examples fascinates you the most? Why?

SITUATION	HOW JESUS SHOWED LOVE
During Jesus' arrest, a disciple struck the servant of the high priest, cutting off his right ear. Jesus healed it (Luke 22:50-52).	Jesus restored an enemy who had been harmed.
At the crucifixion Jesus forgave his executioners on the spot and didn't hold their deeds against them (Luke 23:34).	Jesus forgave his enemies and accepted the circumstances as part of God's larger picture.
Jesus despised the Pharisees' behavior (Matthew 23:37-39; Luke 19:41-44).	Jesus wept that these leaders of Jerusalem would have to suffer so much when Rome later destroyed Jerusalem.
Judas was getting ready to implement his plan to betray Jesus (Matthew 26:50; John 13:3-11).	Jesus called Judas "friend" and washed his feet.

4. *Judgment and condemnation.* What are some other forms of judgment and condemnation besides these?

- Making false assumptions about someone because you don't know them well
- Criticizing someone publicly
- Deciding someone is guilty before you know the true circumstances
- Other:_____

5. In Luke 6:38, Jesus said that as we give, "a good measure, pressed down, shaken together and running over, will be poured into your lap." Picture yourself as someone who has gone to a store or mill to buy flour, cornmeal, or pancake mix. You have brought a container that holds exactly (and only) what you can afford. Buying more would

be ideal, but you can't because you have only a certain amount of money.

So the clerk measures it well and puts it in your container. You are satisfied.

Then the clerk presses it down and shakes it even more so that there is no air whatsoever in the container. You are so really pleased. Then the clerk fills your container running over so that it pours into your lap and you find yourself scooping up the abundant flow into your pockets. You have so much more than you asked for or paid for.

How does it feel to be the recipient of so much generosity?

6. *Fly on the wall cue: Picture the enemy of Jesus' listeners.* If you wish to picture an enemy as this passage is read, choose one of these images to represent them:

- Take the view of the Jews: picture the Romans, Samaritans or any foreign nation.

- Take the view of the disciples: picture the Pharisees.

- Take a personal view and use the face of someone you find difficult.

Now read the passage again—aloud, this time—and close your eyes, picturing the image you selected.

Reflect on the invitation. Perhaps God is offering you an invitation in this passage to enlarge your understanding about something. What might that be? Read the passage again and then sit quietly for a few minutes, pondering these questions:

- What word or phrase stands out to you?

- Why do you think that is?

Reflect a little further. You may wish to read the passage again. As you do this, remember the introduction. Use this time to admire Jesus and how he lived, to let Jesus draw you toward this good and beautiful behavior. Then consider:

- How does this passage connect with your life?

- Is there some idea, feeling or intention you need to embrace from it? If so, what is it?

- What might God be inviting you to be, know, understand, feel or even do?

Be open to the quiet and don't feel pressured to come up with an answer.

RESPOND (*ORATIO*)

Take a few minutes to respond to what you have heard from God. Consider that God is powerful and—if we ask—God can help us take one more step toward becoming the kind of person who is generous and not judgmental. Say what you most wish to say to God about this experience in Scripture.

REST (*CONTEMPLATIO*)

Soak in what has stood out to you in this passage and consider: How did Jesus seem to you in this passage? Remember that this is how God treats you.

Spend a few minutes noticing the thoughts that have come to you. This may take the form of worship or simply resting in God's presence.

TRYING IT ON (*INCARNATIO*)

When you are tempted to judge, set it aside for a while. Instead, smile and move toward the picture of you receiving grace from God, in good measure, pressed down, shaken together and running over, poured into your lap. This is the measure God gives us. Thanks be to God.

Stepping Out in Compassion

Luke 7:11-17

RELAX AND REFOCUS (*SILENCIO*)

Inhale and exhale a few times. Let go of distractions. Quiet your thoughts and open yourself to God.

Optional—If you need more help focusing, ponder this question: What stops me from unhesitatingly stepping out in compassion when I see someone in need?

READ (*LECTIO*)

Read the passage to yourself. Then read the notes below it about the key words and phrases. Consider how these details affect your understanding of the story. Then read the passage aloud slowly. Take time to let the words "fall on your ear."

REFLECT (*MEDITATIO*)

Questions and cues to help you enter into the story.

1. *Cultural background: The life of a widow.* The man who died was the widow's only son. A widow with no sons had no means of support. Perhaps a kind relative might have taken her on in their home. If not, she would have few viable options—some widows even turned to

Luke 7:11-17 (NRSV)

¹¹Soon afterwards he went to a town called Nain, and his disciples and a large crowd went with him. ¹²As he approached the gate of the town, a man who had died was being carried out. He was his mother's only son, and she was a widow; and with her was a large crowd from the town. ¹³When the Lord saw her, he had compassion for her and said to her, "Do not weep." ¹⁴Then he came forward and touched the *bier*, and the bearers stood still. And he said, "Young man, I say to you, *rise*!" ¹⁵The dead man sat up and began to speak, and Jesus gave him to his mother. ¹⁶Fear seized all of them; and they glorified God, saying, "A great prophet has risen among us!" and "God has looked favorably on his people!" ¹⁷This word about him spread *throughout Judea* and all the surrounding country.

bier An open wicker basket used to carry a corpse to its grave, which was usually a small cave where the body was laid out on a shelf until it decomposed.[1] Then the bones would be taken out and deposited in a bone box, leaving the shelf for the next family member.[2]

rise The Greek word, *egeirō* (Strong's 1453), means to waken or rouse. It is closely related to *egersis* (Strong's 1454), which means "resurrection." The disciples may have remembered this when Jesus himself was resurrected.

throughout Judea This incident took place in Galilee but word spread throughout Judea, which was much farther south.

prostitution in their desperation.[3] Her demeaned status seems to have been one reason for Jesus' unhesitating compassion for her.

If you had been in her place, what would you have feared most?

- starvation
- having to beg
- selling all your possessions

What other feelings might you have had?

2. *Fly on the wall cue: Hear the noise of the crowds.* Jesus had a crowd with him (verse 11) and a crowd followed the widow (verse 12), so the

atmosphere would have been filled with noise. "Come inside the story and allow its force to sweep over you. Walk in the crowd a few paces behind the bier, on a hot day in Galilee, with the bright sun sparkling on the tears which are streaming down everyone's cheeks. . . . The professional mourners and wailers are there, making plenty of noise so that friends and relatives, and particularly the poor mother, can cry their hearts out without the embarrassment of making a scene all by themselves."[4]

3. *Purposefulness and certainty.* Jesus helped without hesitation, but if he were like the rest of us, what might have been his reasons to hesitate or not do this miracle at all? (We would, perhaps, call these reasons "common sense.")

- To stay under the radar, since the Pharisees and Herodians were conspiring to destroy him (Mark 3:6).

- Interrupting a funeral is not a courteous thing to do.

- Touching the bier (much less the dead body) would have made Jesus ritually unclean, which would have made him temporarily unable to preach.

- Other:_____

4. What do you think helps people move unhesitatingly to help with compassion?

- Being preoccupied with God and what God cares about.

- Truly seeing others in their situation and feeling empathy for them.

- Other:_____

5. *Fly on the wall cue: Picture the town of Nain.* Because Nain was just five miles from Nazareth,[5] the people of Nazareth would have heard about this incident quickly. They had previously became so enraged

at Jesus' preaching that "they drove him out of the town, and led him to the brow of the hill on which their town was built, so that they might hurl him off the cliff" (Luke 4:29 NRSV). Jesus went on to do many miracles in the area, but even then when he returned to Nazareth, he could "not do many deeds of power there, because of their unbelief" (Matthew 13:58 NRSV).

This might make you wonder what the people of Nazareth thought when, several months later, Jesus brought someone back to life just a few miles away from them. No doubt it was the talk of the town. Did it impress the people of Nazareth?

What do you think?

6. You might picture yourself as one of the people in the passage to take in what happened.

- the widow, who watches her son come back from the dead

- one of those carrying the bier, who was close to Jesus as he did this miracle

- the disciples who watched Jesus barge into this funeral and do the miracle

- someone in the crowd from Nain or visiting from Nazareth

- Other:_____

Reflect on the invitation. Read the passage aloud again. Picture what the scene would look like. Hear the words clearly.

- As you picture the passage, what moment, action or phrase stands out to you?

- As you watch the action, what do you see? What does this cause you to think and feel?

- Why might God have caused that moment, word or phrase to stand out to you?

Reflect a little further.

- How does this passage connect with your life?
- Is there some idea, feeling or intention you need to embrace from it? If so, what is it?
- What might God be inviting you to be, know, understand, feel or even do?

Be open to the quiet and don't feel pressured to come up with an answer.

RESPOND (*ORATIO*)

Take a few minutes to respond about this in prayer. What do you most want to say to Jesus about this experience in Scripture?

REST (*CONTEMPLATIO*)

Soak in what has stood out to you in this passage and consider: How did Jesus (or Jesus' actions and emotions) seem to you in this passage? What does this tell you about what God is like?

Rest for a few minutes in the kind of worship the town of Nain experienced: "They were all filled with awe and praised God. 'A great prophet has appeared among us,' they said. 'God has come to help his people'" (Luke 7:16 NIV). "They all realized they were in a place of holy mystery, that God was at work among them" (Luke 7:16 *The Message*).

TRYING IT ON (*INCARNATIO*)

Ask God to give you an opportunity to reach out in some way without hesitation or fear of any kind.

Cooperating with the Power of God

Ephesians 3:14-21

RELAX AND REFOCUS (*SILENCIO*)

Center yourself by breathing in and out. Relax your neck and take time to let your muscles relax.

Optional—If you need to focus, ponder this question: Who do you know who has true spiritual power for good? Why do you think so? Or if you don't know anyone with spiritual power, what do you think it might look like?

As you quiet yourself, rest your hands in your lap, placing your hands palms down as a symbol of turning over any concerns you have. If a nagging thought or distraction arises, turn your hands palms up as a "symbol of your desire to receive from the Lord."[1] If you become distracted at any time during the meditation, repeat the exercise.

READ (*LECTIO*)

Read the passage to yourself silently. Then read the notes below it about the key words and phrases. Consider how these details help your understanding of the passage. Then read the passage aloud slowly. Take time to let the words "fall on your ear."

Ephesians 3:14-21

¹⁴*For this reason* I kneel before the Father, **¹⁵**from whom every family in heaven and on earth derives its name. **¹⁶**I pray that out of his glorious riches he may strengthen you with power through his Spirit in your inner being, **¹⁷**so that Christ may dwell in your hearts through faith. And I pray that you, being rooted and established in love, **¹⁸**may have power, together with all the Lord's holy people, to grasp how wide and long and high and deep is the love of Christ, **¹⁹**and to know this love that surpasses knowledge—that you may be filled to the measure of all the fullness of God.

²⁰Now to him who is able to do immeasurably more than all we ask or imagine, according to his power that is at work within us, **²¹**to him be ***glory*** in the church and in Christ Jesus throughout all generations, for ever and ever! Amen.

For this reason Paul has just written about God's plan to build a worldwide community and heavenly family, which is the church. Paul seems to be in such awe of this plan that he kneels to pray.
glory The manifestation of God's goodness, beauty, power and truth.

Reflect (*MEDITATIO*)

Questions and cues to help you reflect on the passage.

1. Underline the word *love* in the passage. It occurs three times. Circle the word *power* in the passage, which also occurs three times.

   What about love in this passage is most intriguing to you? What about power is most intriguing?

2. *If Paul went to your church.* Try to paraphrase a few of Paul's lofty phrases, putting them in everyday language that might resonate a little more with people in your church. (This may rob the language of some of its beauty and majesty, but it may also help you get your head around it a bit better.)

NIV	The Message	NLT	Your own paraphrase
his glorious riches		his glorious, unlimited resources	
strengthen you with power through his Spirit in your inner being,	strengthen you by his Spirit—not a brute strength but a glorious inner strength	give you mighty inner strength through his Holy Spirit	
Christ may dwell in your hearts through faith.	Christ will live in you as you open the door and invite him in	Christ will be more and more at home in your hearts as you trust in him.	
being rooted and established in love,	with both feet planted firmly on love,	have the power to understand, as all God's people should, how wide, how long, how high, and how deep his love really is	
may have power to grasp how wide and long and high and deep is the love of Christ	take in with all Christians the extravagant dimensions of Christ's love		
[power to] know this love that surpasses knowledge	Live full lives,	May you experience the love of Christ, though it is so great you will never fully understand it.	
be filled to the measure of all the fullness of God.	full in the fullness of God.	filled with fullness of life and power that comes from God.	

3. *Prayer and study.* Paul's letters are full of instruction about doctrine and how to think about God. But his instruction flows in and around the many prayers that are also part of the letters. "Perhaps the best Christian doctrine is that which emerges from the life of prayer. Better that way round than an arid intellectual exploration coupled with some perfunctory acts of worship."[2]

Why is it important for us to combine our study with prayer, and prayer with study?

4. *Spiritual power.* The upside-down values of the kingdom (for example, the last will be first, and the first will be last) mean that the way the

world looks at things is different from the kingdom view. Here's a possible view of how the world looks at things, with positional power being the highest form of authority.

1. Positional power	People listen to you because you hold a position, role, office or title. They may or may not actually respect you, but they're required to submit to you.
2. Expert power	People listen to you because you know a lot about a certain topic. You have information they want. When you stop giving information, they may stop listening.
3. Relational power	People listen to you because they treasure you as a person, and they treasure their relationship with you. They know you and your character.
4. Spiritual power	People listen to you because they can tell that you know God. They get a sense of God speaking to them through you. This is the strongest kind of power or authority. No one *has* to listen to you, respect you or follow what you say. They do it because they see God in you.

How might these four types of power be valued in the kingdom of God?

5. What are the signs that a person has *spiritual* power? (These types of power aren't exclusive. You may know some people who have all four kinds of power.)

- They trust God more in situations that used to bother them.

- They love people (instead of tolerating them).

- They are aware that God is working within them in exciting ways even when life seems ho-hum.

- Other:_____

6. *Seek power, not position.* Seeking power is different from seeking position. This prayer seems to be urging us to seek spiritual power. Elsewhere Scripture warns about seeking a high position, such as the important seat at the table. We are not to seek others' adulation, or

try to be in charge (Matthew 23:6). The lowest seat is fine (Luke 14:8-11). Holding a position of authority is not wrong, but it is wrong to set our hearts on it. Hoping for position crowds out our simple task of following God today and of living our lives in the kingdom today. It crowds out contentment.

How do you feel about the idea of God giving you spiritual power?

- I'm not sure.

- I'm not ready for this.

- It would be good if I had the good character to go with it.

- I long to be used by God more.

- Other:_____

Reflect on the invitation. Read the passage again and then sit quietly for a few minutes, pondering these questions:

- What word or phrase stands out to you?

- Why do you think that is?

Reflect a little further. You may wish to read the passage again. As you do this, remember the introduction. Use this time to admire Jesus and how he lived, and to let Jesus draw you toward this good and beautiful behavior. Then consider:

- How does this passage connect with your life?

- Is there some idea, feeling or intention you need to embrace from it? If so, what is it?

- What might God be inviting you to be, know, understand, feel or even do?

Be open to the quiet and don't feel pressured to come up with an answer.

Respond (*ORATIO*)

Take a few minutes to respond to whatever has come to you. Say what you most wish to say to God about this experience in Scripture.

You may wish to ask God questions (the answers to which may come to you later). You may wish to write your prayer down. Sometimes that keeps our mind from wandering.

Rest (*CONTEMPLATIO*)

Soak in what has stood out to you in this passage and consider: How might you rest in God's glory—God's goodness, beauty, power and truth—as evident to you?

Spend a few minutes noticing the thoughts that have come to you. This may take the form of worship or simply resting in God's presence.

Trying It On (*INCARNATIO*)

Pray the prayer in this passage for several days. First, pray it for yourself. Then pray it for others, especially someone you want to have spiritual power.

37

Responding to the Passion
God Puts in Our Hearts

Nehemiah 1–2

RELAX AND REFOCUS (*SILENCIO*)

Center yourself by breathing in and out. Relax your neck and breathe out again. Let your shoulders relax.

Optional—If you need help focusing, think of someone you have admired who has a passion to make a difference.

READ (*LECTIO*)

Read the passage to yourself. Then read the notes below it about the key words and phrases. Consider how these details affect your understanding of the story. Then read the passage aloud slowly. Take time to let the words "fall on your ear."

REFLECT (*MEDITATIO*)

Questions and cues to help you enter into the story.

1. *Nehemiah the Jewish politician from Persia.* Nehemiah would have lived his entire life in Babylon or in Susa, the capital of Persia. He had an important job in the Persian government that commanded a

lot of respect. Still, his Jewish homeland meant a lot to him, making it easy for God to put the burden of Jerusalem's welfare on his heart.

What people or group of people are experiencing brokenness and break your heart when you ponder them—even if they are remote?

In what area of your life do you feel like an exile, estranged from who you are and the purposes God has for you?

2. *Nehemiah the leader.* Nehemiah paid attention to "what my God had put in my heart to do" (2:12). This strong sense of purpose is evident by the following items:

- his weeping over his homeland
- his inspection of the walls by night
- his emphasis on the "gracious hand of God" (2:8, 18)
- his powerful persuasion of the officials

How do the first two items differ from useless brooding?

3. Nehemiah's passion showed in the way he wept, prayed and followed through with his plan. How do the following actions (that Nehemiah experienced and did) build passion in people?

- experiencing others' brokenness and helping in tangible ways
- praying for God's wisdom and insight
- confessing a lack of faithfulness in the past
- doing a task, even if it's insignificant, to help the broken situation

4. *Fly on the wall cue: Picture life in Persia for Nehemiah.* Because Nehemiah held an important rank, he probably lived well and had assistants waiting on him. He probably worked and lived in the two palaces of King Artaxerxes I. Besides the summer palace in Susa, the winter palace in Persepolis had a flat terrace with seventy-two great columns, topped by carvings of bulls and horned lions. The palace and

Nehemiah 1–2

(1:2-4, 6, 11; 2:2-4, 8, 11-12, 15, 17-18)

1:²Hanani, one of my brothers, came from Judah with some other men, and I questioned them about the *Jewish remnant that had survived the exile*, and also about Jerusalem. ³They said to me, "Those who survived the exile and are *back in the province* are in great trouble and disgrace. The wall of Jerusalem is broken down, and its gates have been *burned with fire*."

⁴When I heard these things, *I sat down and wept*. For some days I mourned and fasted and prayed before the God of heaven. . . .

⁶"I confess the sins we Israelites, including myself and my father's family, have committed against you. . . ."

¹¹I was *cupbearer* to the king.

2:²*The king* asked me, "Why does your face look so sad when you are not ill? This can be nothing but sadness of heart." I was very *much afraid*, ³but I said to the king, "May the king live forever! Why should my face not look sad when the city where my ancestors are buried lies in ruins, and its gates have been destroyed by fire?" ⁴The king said to me, "What is it you want?"

Then I *prayed to the God of heaven* . . . ⁸And because the gracious hand of my God was on me, the king granted *my requests*.

Jewish remnant that had survived the exile Throughout Israel's history God warned that Israel would be taken captive by another nation if they continued to live wickedly and worship idols. Judah, the southern kingdom, was taken into exile by Babylonia in 586 BC. A few Israelites were left behind. Since then Babylon had been conquered by Cyrus, king of Persia, in whose court Nehemiah served.
back in the province After seventy years two waves of exiles had returned, led by Zerubbabel and Ezra.
burned with fire The Babylonians had besieged and burned Jerusalem. A small group had since tried to rebuild the walls, but the neighboring Samaritans stopped them.
I sat down and wept Nehemiah lived in exile in Persia, far from his Jewish homeland. He cared about Jerusalem's welfare and his love for his homeland is on display throughout this book.
cupbearer This position was something like the US Secret Service, which protects the president. Nehemiah taste-tested the king's food and drink to foil assassination plots. He had to be completely trustworthy, above taking a bribe.

[11]I went to Jerusalem, and after staying there three days [12]I set out during the night with a few others. I had not told anyone what my God had put in my heart to do for Jerusalem. . . . [15]So I went up the valley by night, examining the wall.

[17]Then I said to them, "You see the trouble we are in: Jerusalem lies in ruins, and its gates have been burned with fire. Come, let us rebuild the wall of Jerusalem, and we will no longer be in disgrace." [18]I also told them about the gracious hand of my God on me and what the king had said to me. They replied, "Let us start rebuilding." So they began this good work.

the king King Artaxerxes I of Persia (Nehemiah 2:1).
much afraid No matter how trusted they were, servants did not bother the king with their problems, nor did they make bold requests for permission and provisions for a cause their master had already outlawed (Ezra 4:17-22).
prayed to the God of heaven Nehemiah can be found praying in all kinds of situations throughout this narrative.
my requests Nehemiah requested a leave of absence for himself, letters to the governors of provinces for safe travel through their territories, a requisition letter for timber to build with. The king also sent army officers and horsemen to protect Nehemiah.

city were surrounded by three separate walls carved with elaborate figures and protected by many watchtowers.[1] How might Nehemiah have felt in the uncivilized wild west outpost of Jerusalem with its crumbled walls?

Here are some scenes you might choose to picture:

- Weeping for the homeland: Imagine Nehemiah asking the Jews specifically about the welfare of the people in Jerusalem and what the city looked like.

- Interacting with the king (four months later): Imagine Nehemiah's fear as he risked personal and political rejection.

- Inspecting the walls: Imagine Nehemiah going by night with just a few men to survey the damage.

- Offering the vision to the officials in Jerusalem: The king of Persia had championed this idea, which was a miracle. But the people of Jerusalem felt hopeless. How did the officials in this outland province view Nehemiah, who may have behaved more like a Persian than a Jew? Had these officials resigned themselves to the condition of the broken walls? One attempt to rebuild them had already failed, so they may have thought: *Who does this guy Nehemiah think he is? Why does he bother?* Did they resent him as a representative of an oppressive world power?

Reflect on the invitation. Read the passage aloud again. Picture what the scene would have looked like. Hear the words clearly.

- As you picture the passage, what moment, action or phrase stands out to you?

- As you watch the action, what do you see? What does this cause you to think and feel?

- Why might God have caused that moment, word or phrase to stand out to you?

Reflect a little further.

- How does this passage connect with your life?

- Is there some idea, feeling or intention you need to embrace from it? If so, what is it?

- What might God be inviting you to be, know, understand, feel or even do?

Be open to the quiet and don't feel pressured to come up with an answer.

RESPOND (*ORATIO*)

Take a few minutes to respond to God about this. What do you most want to say to God about this experience in Scripture?

REST (*CONTEMPLATIO*)

Soak in what has stood out to you in this passage and consider: How did God's actions or partnership with Nehemiah seem to you in this passage? What does this tell you about what God is like?

Spend a few minutes noticing the thoughts that have come to you. This may take the form of worship or simply resting in God's presence.

TRYING IT ON (*INCARNATIO*)

Consider this question: What breaks your heart that also breaks the heart of God? Ask God for a next step.

38

Relating to God in Failure

Matthew 14:22-33

RELAX AND REFOCUS (*SILENCIO*)

Center yourself by breathing in and out. Relax your neck and breathe out again. Let your shoulders relax.

Optional—If you need to focus, ponder this question: How do you think God views failures?

READ (*LECTIO*)

Read the passage to yourself. Then read the notes below it about the key words and phrases. Consider how these details affect your understanding of the story. Then read the passage aloud slowly. Take time to let the words "fall on your ear."

REFLECT (*MEDITATIO*)

1. *Fly on the wall cue: Picture Jesus coming toward you on the sea.* In the wind, rain and rough sea, the disciples would have had difficulty seeing the ghostly figure of Jesus coming toward them over the sea (John 6:18).

2. *Fly on the wall cue: Picture the disciples.* Even though several disciples were professional fishermen, they seemed to find the conditions

Matthew 14:22-33

²²Immediately Jesus made the disciples get into the boat and go on ahead of him to the other side, while he dismissed the crowd. ²³After he had dismissed them, he went up on a mountainside by himself to pray. Later that night, he was there alone, ²⁴and the boat was already a considerable distance from land, buffeted by the waves because the wind was against it.

²⁵Shortly before dawn Jesus went out to them, walking on the lake. ²⁶When the disciples saw him walking on the lake, they were terrified. "It's a ghost," they said, and cried out in fear.

²⁷But Jesus immediately said to them: "Take courage! It is I. **Don't be afraid.**"

²⁸"Lord, if it's you," Peter replied, "tell me to come to you on the water."

²⁹"Come," he said.

Then Peter got down out of the boat, walked on the water and came toward Jesus.³⁰But when he saw the wind, he was afraid and, beginning to sink, cried out, "Lord, save me!"

³¹Immediately Jesus reached out his hand and caught him. "You of little faith," he said, "why did you doubt?"

³²And when they climbed into the boat, the wind died down. ³³Then those who were in the boat worshiped him, saying, "Truly you are the Son of God."

Immediately Jesus had just fed a group of five thousand men and their families. The disciples seem to have been stunned and unsure how that happened. When Jesus realized the people were about to come and take him by force to make him king, he put the disciples on a boat and withdrew to the mountain by himself (John 6:15).
Don't be afraid N. T. Wright postulates that the disciples were "caught between glory and terror" when they saw Jesus walking on the lake.[1]

challenging and even frightening. The disciples were probably sweating from the strain of hard rowing, but cold from the wind and waves.

Put yourself in the place of the disciples struggling at the oars in turbulent water and hearing the howling wind. What would they have seen or heard? What were they touching? Were their hands bloodied? How would their bodies have felt?

What were they feeling?

- terror

- weariness

- despair

- Other:_____

3. *Jesus' motives.* Why do you think Jesus walked on water that night?

- Jesus was a compassionate person, and his miracles were very personal. He could have calmed the storm from the shore, but he came to where they were to help.[2]

- Jesus was always near and wanted them to know this. This is much like Jesus' unexpected post-resurrection appearances, when he showed up unexpectedly. As Leslie Weatherhead puts it, perhaps Jesus was "making them feel that He is never far away. He does not seem to be there. Then He breaks in upon them, always knows what has happened, always takes charge of the situation, until they never know when they may become aware of Him. They must often have turned at the opening of a door expecting to see Himself. They stopped midway in a sentence because they remembered that He could not be far away. . . . They feel that He is never absent."[3]

- Other:_____

4. *Character focus: Giving Peter a break.* We're often hard on Peter, but notice he's the only disciple who walked on water. Peter saw what his master was doing and wanted to join him. N. T. Wright asks, "Would you rather have a friend who did what seemed the right thing and

then worried about it later, or one who spent so much time thinking it all through that it would take weeks to get anything done?"[4]

5. *"You of little faith."* Some people assume that Jesus' question, "You of little faith, why did you doubt?" was a disparaging remark, perhaps even a scolding. "You of little faith" is one Greek word, *oligopistos*, meaning "little faith." It appears to be a word Jesus made up, a sort of nickname for his disciples when he wanted them to expand their thinking.[5] Consider that each time he used it, he was challenging them to do something that most people don't do, or something that was difficult to believe. For example, he was asking them

- not to worry about where tomorrow's meal would come from (Matthew 6:30);

- not to be surprised that he could talk to the wind and make it calm (Matthew 8:26);

- not to be surprised that a person could walk on water (Matthew 14:31);

- not to be concerned when it's time to eat, but there's no food (Matthew 16:8); and

- to remove a raging demon from a badly disabled boy's body (Matthew 17:8).

In truth, all of us are *oligopistos*. Do you think Jesus was the kind of person who got exasperated when people are *not* full of superhuman faith?

6. If Jesus was instead patient, kind and not easily irritated (1 Corinthians 13:4-5) with the disciples, yet still challenged them, what might have been the look on his face when he reached out to catch Peter?

- annoyed, rolling his eyes

- disappointed that Peter had fallen

- concerned for Peter's welfare

- grinning to reassure Peter that he would not drown
- Other:_____

7. *Jesus as teacher.* Jesus' movement was quick—immediately reaching out his hand to catch Peter. As Peter's teacher, Jesus responded to his apprentice who ventured out on dangerous waves with him. Most teachers enjoy the antics of their most adventurous students. Perhaps Jesus was the kind of teacher who often gave his disciples a chance to experiment (Luke 9:1-6). He often rescued them when they didn't have the astonishing faith they would later have (Mark 9:14-21). On this occasion Jesus gave Peter an especially long leash, letting Peter imitate his own unbelievable behavior. After Peter's short success and failure, he wisely called out to Jesus, who was within arm's reach, as a good teacher would be. A good teacher often says, "Try something wild. I'll catch you."[6]

Reflect on the invitation. Read the passage aloud again. Enter into the scene, considering how the disciples would have felt and what they saw and heard. Hear the words clearly.

Perhaps you will see yourself as Peter, or as a disciple who was horrified that Peter tried this, or as a disciple who envied Peter for trying.

- As you picture the events of the passage, what moment, action or phrase is most real to you? What does this cause you to think and feel?

- Why might that moment, word or phrase have stood out to you?

Reflect a little further.

- How does this passage connect with your life?

- Is there some idea, feeling or intention you need to embrace from it? If so, what is it?

- What might God be inviting you to be, know, understand, feel or even do?

Be open to the quiet and don't feel pressured to come up with an answer.

RESPOND (*ORATIO*)

Take a few minutes to respond to God about this. What do you most want to say to God about this experience in Scripture? You might want to ask God about failure and how God responds to failure—especially one of your failures. You might want to ask Jesus to show you how he responded to Peter's bold action and subsequent failure.

REST (*CONTEMPLATIO*)

Soak in what has stood out to you in this passage and consider how Jesus (or Jesus' words and actions) seemed to you in this passage. What does this tell you about what God is like?

Spend a few more minutes noticing the thoughts that have come to you. Immerse yourself in the response of the disciples: They worshiped him, saying, "Truly you are the Son of God."

TRYING IT ON (*INCARNATIO*)

Ask God for courage to venture out a little more and see what happens. What might the "water" be that you want to walk on by God's power?

Drinking the Cup of Suffering

Matthew 20:20-28

RELAX AND REFOCUS (*SILENCIO*)

Center yourself by breathing in and out. Relax your neck and breathe out again. Let your shoulders relax.

Optional—If you need to focus, ponder this idea: Many of us want to be can-do, go-getter types of people. God wants us to "become broken bread and poured out wine in the hands of Jesus Christ."[1]

READ (*LECTIO*)

Read the passage to yourself. Then read the notes below it about the key words and phrases. Consider how these details affect your understanding of the story. Then read the passage aloud slowly. Take time to let the words "fall on your ear."

REFLECT (*MEDITATIO*)

Questions and cues to help you enter into the story.

1. *The great inversion: The "great" are servants.* James, John and their mother all assumed that power in the kingdom looked like political power on earth. Jesus was clear that his kingdom does not operate like that. "You know that the rulers of the Gentiles lord it over them, and their high officials exercise authority over them. Not so with you"

Matthew 20:20-28

20Then the mother of **Zebedee's sons** came to Jesus with her sons and, kneeling down, asked a favor of him.

21"What is it you want?" he asked.

She said, "Grant that one of these two sons of mine may **sit at your right and the other at your left** in your kingdom."

22"You don't know what you are asking," Jesus said to them. "Can you drink **the cup** I am going to drink?"

"We can," they answered.

23Jesus said to them, "You will indeed drink from my cup, but to sit at my right or left is not for me to grant. These places belong to those for whom they have been prepared by my Father."

24When the ten heard about this, they were indignant with the two brothers. **25**Jesus called them together and said, "You know that the rulers of the Gentiles lord it over them, and their high officials exercise authority over them. **26**Not so with you. Instead, whoever wants to become great among you must be your servant, **27**and whoever wants to be first must be your slave—**28**just as the Son of Man did not come to be served, but to serve, and to give his life as a ransom for many."

Zebedee's sons The apostles, James and John, whom Jesus nicknamed the "sons of thunder" (Mark 3:17). Elsewhere they wanted to call down fire from heaven on some Samaritans who wouldn't receive Christ (Luke 9:54).

sit at your right and the other at your left These were positions of power and prestige—they were asking to be Jesus' closest advisers in what they supposed would be his earthly kingdom.

the cup Jesus seems to be referring to his suffering and crucifixion (see Matthew 26:39, 42; Jeremiah 25:15-38; Mark 14:36; Luke 22:42; John 18:11).

(Matthew 20:25-26). Instead, the great in the kingdom are servants of others (verses 26-27).

Who do you know (if anyone) who is "great" in your eyes and also a servant of others? Why do you view them as great?

2. *Character focus: James, John and their mother.* According to the parallel passage (Mark 10:35), James and John asked for the position themselves—their desire for elevated positions was theirs as well as their mother's. That desire is a common one with which we can identify. Most of us like having people look up to us and think we're important.

The cup they would drink (verse 23) was a cup of suffering. Their mother got a close-up glimpse of the cup of suffering at the crucifixion (Matthew 27:54-56). Perhaps she understood then the cup of suffering that awaited her sons. Later, James would be martyred and John would be exiled (Acts 12:2; Revelation 1:9).

3. *Fly on the wall cue: Picture how the timing affected the conversation.* This discussion occurred not long before Jesus' death. The disciples were on their way to Jerusalem, where Jesus' enemies were looking to kill him. Because the showdown was imminent, these three may have thought this was their last chance to approach Jesus. Their requests created a rousing discussion among the disciples. Jesus would respond that greatness is about being a servant (Matthew 20:26-28).

4. Why might the disciples have been so disturbed?

- Some wished they'd thought to ask the same question.

- Some understood that greatness is about servanthood, just from watching Jesus, and were thus annoyed at James and John.

- Other:_____

Reflect on the invitation. Read the passage aloud again. Imagine yourself in the place of James, John, their mother or one of the other disciples. See James and John's mother kneeling before Jesus, asking for this favor. Picture Jesus' shocking reply that even though Gentile rulers lorded authority over others, it would not be so among them.

- As you picture the events of the passage, what moment, action or phrase is most real to you? What does this cause you to think and feel?

- Why might that moment, word or phrase have stood out to you? *Reflect a little further.*

- How does this passage connect with your life?

- Is there some idea, feeling or intention you need to embrace from it? If so, what is it?

- What might God be inviting you to be, know, understand, feel or even do?

- Perhaps God is asking you the two questions in the passage:

  - "What is it you want?" Answer this truthfully and candidly, not necessarily with the answer you think God wants to hear.

  - "Can you drink the cup I am going to drink?"

Be open to the quiet and don't feel pressured to come up with an answer.

Respond (*ORATIO*)

Take a few minutes to respond to God about this. You might need to ask God questions about this or for help to embrace these ideas.

Rest (*CONTEMPLATIO*)

Perhaps you find this passage unsettling and wonder how you are supposed to rest after reading such a grim passage. With good reason. Consider the face of Jesus during this conversation. He either knew or could have guessed that his followers would suffer a similar fate to his. Even though he was honest with them, which would help them live in the reality of their imminent persecution, he did not chide them for their inability to understand or their prideful ambition, nor did he question their loyalty.

Jesus seemed to know that they would follow him and that they would also suffer. In spite of their current blindness and arrogance, they would willingly drink the cup. William Barclay writes that Jesus "believed that they could and would drink the cup, and that in the end they would still be found at His side. One of the great fundamental facts to which we must hold on, even when we hate and loathe and despise ourselves, is that Jesus Christ believes in us."[2]

Spend a few minutes noticing the thoughts that come to you from this passage. This may take the form of worship or simply resting in God's presence.

TRYING IT ON (*INCARNATIO*)

Ask God to show you a situation in which you can experiment with taking the self-giving, sacrificial path instead of the self-serving one.

Doing Nothing on My Own

Proverbs 3:5-8

RELAX AND REFOCUS (*SILENCIO*)

Center yourself by breathing in and out. Relax your neck and take time to let your muscles relax.

Optional—If you need to focus, ponder this question: When have you tried to figure something out on your own and it didn't work? If there was someone who came alongside you and helped you, how did that feel? If not, how would it have felt?

READ (*LECTIO*)

Read the passage to yourself silently. Then read the notes below it about the key words and phrases. Consider how these details help your understanding of the passage. Then read the passage aloud slowly. Take time to let the words "fall on your ear."

REFLECT (*MEDITATIO*)

Questions and cues to help you reflect on the passage.

1. *Life on our own (being wise in our own eyes).*

   Life is inner power to reach and live "beyond." Human life cannot flourish as God intended it to, in a divinely inspired and upheld

Proverbs 3:5-8 (ESV)

[5]Trust in the LORD with all your **heart**
    and do not lean on your own understanding;
[6]in all your ways **acknowledge** him,
    and he will make straight your paths.
[7]Be not wise in your own eyes;
    fear the LORD and turn away from evil.
[8]It will be healing to your flesh
    and refreshment to your bones.

Proverbs 3:5-8
(*The Message*)

[5]Trust GOD from the bottom of your **heart**;
    don't try to figure out everything on your own.
[6]Listen for GOD's voice in everything you do, everywhere you go;
    he's the one who will keep you on track.
[7]Don't assume that you know it all.
    Run to GOD! Run from evil!
[8]Your body will glow with health,
    your very bones will vibrate with life!

---

heart The center of our being, which is our spirit (Dallas Willard describes it as "un-bodily personal power"), which includes our choices (our will). The part of you that makes you "you."[1]
acknowledge The Hebrew word, *yada* (Strong's 3045), means to know, in the sense of being acquainted with or interacting with.

corporate rule over this grand globe, if we see ourselves as "on our own"—and especially if we struggle to preserve ourselves that way. When we are in isolation from God and not in the proper social bonds with others, we cannot rule the earth for good—the idea is simply absurd.[2]

In what situations, circumstances or relationships are you most likely to live life on your own? Why do you think that is?

- Trying to conform to what others want you to do or be.

- Trying to achieve something.

- Moving through grief, rejection or failure.

- Feeling secure in material things, relationships and health.

- Other:_____

2. *Jesus did nothing on his own.* "Listen to the words Jesus uses to speak of His relationship to the Father, and how unceasingly He uses the words *not* and *nothing* in reference to Himself.

- "The Son can do *nothing* by Himself" (John 5:19).

- "I can do *nothing* by Myself. My judgment is just because I do *not* seek My own will" (John 5:30).

- "I do *not* receive praise from men" (John 5:41).

- "I have *not* come to do My own will" (John 6:38).

- "My teaching is *not* My own" (John 7:16).

- "I am *not* here on My own" (John 7:28).

- "I do *nothing* on My own" (John 8:28).

- "I have *not* come on My own, but He sent Me" (John 8:42).

- "I do *not* seek glory for Myself" (John 8:50).

- "The words that I say are *not* just My own" (John 14:10).

- "These words you hear are *not* My own" (John 14:24).

These words of Jesus open us up to understand the deepest roots of Christ's life and work. They tell us how it was that the Almighty God was able to work His mighty redemptive work through Him."[3]

How do you respond to such dependence on God by Jesus? Are you

- Surprised that Jesus depended on God?
- Puzzled that Jesus needed (or wanted) to depend on God?
- Impressed by Jesus' submission to God?
- Other:_____

3. *God as loving partner.* Andrew Murray writes that "The love of the Father to the Son is not a sentiment—it is a divine life, an infinite energy, an irresistible power. . . . So the love of Christ to us too is an infinite living power that will work in us all He delights to give us."[4] We are invited to "participate in this divine nature" (2 Peter 1:4).

How might the life described in these verses result in healed flesh and a refreshed body (Proverbs 3:8)?

4. *Passage remixed.* Try paraphrasing Proverbs 3:5-8, emphasizing how we can depend on God every minute (verse 6).

New International Version	Your Paraphrase
[5]Trust in the LORD with all your heart, and lean not on your own understanding.	
[6]In all your ways submit to him, and he will make your paths straight.	
[7]Do not be wise in your own eyes; fear the LORD, and shun evil.	
[8]This will bring health to your body and nourishment to your bones.	

Reflect on the invitation. Perhaps God is offering you an invitation in this passage to enlarge your understanding about something. What might that be? Read the passage again and then sit quietly for a few minutes, pondering these questions:

- What word or phrase stands out to you?

- Why do you think that is?

Reflect a little further. You may wish to read the passage again. Then consider:

- How does this passage connect with your life?

- Is there some idea, feeling or intention you need to embrace from it? If so, what is it?

- What might God be inviting you to be, know, understand, feel or even do?

Be open to the quiet and don't feel pressured to come up with an answer.

Respond (*ORATIO*)

Take a few minutes to respond to what you have heard from God. Say what you most wish to say to God about this experience in Scripture.

Rest (*CONTEMPLATIO*)

Soak in what has stood out to you in this passage and whatever invitation may have come to you. Consider what it would feel like to trust God "with all your heart"—with everything that is within you.

Spend a few minutes noticing the thoughts that have come to you. This may take the form of worship or simply resting in God's presence.

Trying It On (*INCARNATIO*)

Pick a situation in which you would like to depend on God in a greater way. Ask God to show you what that might look like and then try it out.

How to Meditate on Your Own

You may find the Spirit leading you to meditate on many other Scripture passages. Here are some ideas that might help.

Try to focus on ten verses or less. More than that can become complicated. It can get harder to truly hear and focus on. If a passage is much longer, meditate on it in ten-verse increments over a few days. Meditating on small portions fights against the "achievement" attitude we often have about Bible reading, in which the goal is to finish the chapter or to get to the bottom of the page. The goal in lectio is simply to be present to God in Scripture and allow God to communicate to us whatever we most need to hear. In lectio we engage deeply in the text instead of just covering a section or chapter.

Meditate as you can, not as you can't. If something about lectio doesn't work for you, do it the way it does work for you. In that case, you might later revisit what generally works to see if you've grown more used to the rhythm of it. In the meantime, trust God to lead you in how best to tweak the process.

Choosing a passage. Choose a topic that God is speaking to you about or a passage that you need to embrace deeply. This is especially true when starting out. This book is arranged topically to help you do that. You may find that the lectio process takes more time than you usually have, so you might want to do it less frequently. You may want to stay in the same passage for several days. Dietrich Bonhoeffer gave his seminary students at Finkenwalde the same passage for a week to meditate on. He told them that they couldn't use their commentaries during that time because they were reading to interact with God.[1]

Do preparatory work when meditating on a passage that is unfamiliar to you. You may want to study its background or read it in several versions. If a pastor's sermon provides that for you, you might want to meditate on the preached text during the week.

Let go of expectations. Allow yourself to be surprised. Bonhoeffer wrote:

> Let none expect from silence anything but a direct encounter with the Word of God, for the sake of which he has entered into silence. But this encounter will be given to him. The Christian will not lay down conditions as to what he expects or hopes to get from this encounter. If he will simply accept it, his silence will be richly rewarded.[2]

Acknowledgments

I'm thankful for the students and retreat participants who gave me feedback about what worked and what didn't work in these meditation exercises—especially those I assisted in Dallas Willard's Fuller Seminary class, "Spirituality and Ministry," from 2002 to 2012.

As always, I'm forever grateful to my husband, Greg, who is the final reader of all my manuscripts. He keeps my writing down-to-earth but is still willing to run alongside me in my adventurous moments.

Notes

INTRODUCTION

¹In adding *silencio* and *incarnatio* I'm following the lead of the late Robert Mulholland in his book *Invitation to a Journey: A Road Map for Spiritual Formation* (Downers Grove, IL: InterVarsity Press, 1993), 113.

²Richard Foster, *Celebration of Discipline* (San Francisco: Harper & Row, 1988), 30-31.

³Dietrich Bonhoeffer, *Life Together* (New York: Harper & Row, 1954), 82.

⁴Dallas Willard, *Hearing God: Developing a Conversational Relationship with God* (Downers Grove, IL: InterVarsity Press, 2012), 239.

⁵Revised from the "Introduction to the Talk" in Epiphany Ministry, www .epiphanyministry.org.

WHY MEDITATE ON SCRIPTURE?

¹Psalm 1:2; 19:14; 39:3; 48:9; 77:12; 104:34; 119:15, 23, 27, 48, 78, 97, 99, 148; 143:5; 145:5.

CHAPTER 1: KNOWING GOD AS LOVE (1 CORINTHIANS 13:4-8)

¹Dallas Willard defines *agapē* love as the "will to good or 'bene-volence.' We love something or someone when we promote their good for their own sake." Dallas Willard, *Renovation of the Heart* (Colorado Springs, CO: NavPress, 2002), 130.

²Tom Wright, *Paul for Everyone: 1 Corinthians* (Louisville, KY: Westminster John Knox Press, 2004), 8.

CHAPTER 2: SOUGHT AFTER, NO MATTER WHAT (LUKE 15:1-7)

[1]Kenneth E. Bailey, *The Good Shepherd: A Thousand-Year Journey from Psalm 23 to the New Testament* (Downers Grove, IL: IVP Academic, 2014), 110-11.

[2]William Barclay, *The Daily Bible Study: The Gospel of Luke* (Philadelphia: Westminster Press, 1956), 206.

[3]Bailey, *Good Shepherd*, 140.

[4]Phillip Keller, *A Shepherd Looks at Psalm 23* (Grand Rapids: Zondervan, 1970), 60-61.

CHAPTER 4: GOD'S COMPASSION FOR THE REBELLIOUS (LUKE 15:11-24)

[1]Kenneth E. Bailey, *Jesus Through Middle Eastern Eyes: Cultural Studies in the Gospels* (Downers Grove, IL: IVP Academic, 2008), 177.

[2]J. A. Thompson, *Handbook of Life in Bible Times* (Leicester, UK: Inter-Varsity Press, 1986), 105.

CHAPTER 5: GOD'S COMPASSION FOR THE OUTWARDLY COMPLIANT (LUKE 15:25-32)

[1]David Benner, *Surrender to Love* (Downers Grove, IL: InterVarsity Press, 2003), 15.

[2]Dallas Willard, "Spiritual Formation as a Natural Part of Salvation," presented at the 2009 Wheaton Theology Conference, www.dwillard .org/articles/artview.asp?artID=135.

[3]Henri J. M. Nouwen, *The Return of the Prodigal Son* (New York: Doubleday, 1992), 131.

CHAPTER 6: BLESSED WITH EVERY BLESSING (EPHESIANS 1:3-14)

[1]Translation by Tom Wright, *Paul for Everyone: The Prison Letters* (Louisville, KY: Westminster John Knox Press, 2004), 7.

[2]Ibid.

CHAPTER 7: ONE IN WHOM CHRIST DWELLS (EPHESIANS 2:13-22)

[1]I heard this definition from Dallas Willard in a Renovaré Institute lecture, St. Malo Retreat Center, Allenspark, Colorado, March 15, 2011, day one, lecture three.

[2]As David Benner writes, "In Roman times, the *templa* was a particular segment of the heavens, the place where God dwelled." From "Being with God: The Practice of Contemplative Prayer," *Conversations Journal* 4, vol. 2 (Fall 2006): 6-7.

[3]N. T. Wright, *Simply Christian* (New York: HarperCollins, 2006), 63-64, 81.

THE "SANCTIFIED" IMAGINATION

[1]John Mogabgab, editor's introduction, *Weavings* 12, no. 1 (Jan/Feb 1997): 2-3.

CHAPTER 9: LIFE IN THE SPIRIT (ROMANS 8:1-11, 14)

[1]Tom Wright, *Paul for Everyone: Romans Part 1: Chapters 1–8* (Louisville, KY: Westminster John Knox Press, 2004), 141-42.

[2]Dallas Willard, *Renovation of the Heart* (Colorado Springs, CO: Nav-Press, 2002), 164.

[3]Ibid., 65.

[4]Paraphrased from Wright, *Paul for Everyone: Romans Part 1,* 142.

[5]Wright, *Paul for Everyone: Romans Part 1,* 140.

CHAPTER 10: BLESSED TO BE A BLESSING (GENESIS 12:1-5; 21:1-7)

[1]"Child, Children," in *International Standard Bible Encyclopedia*, vol. 1 (Grand Rapids: Eerdmans, 1939), 606. See also "Relationships, Family," vol. 4, p. 2554.

CHAPTER 11: RELYING ON THE KINGDOM OF GOD (MATTHEW 6:10, 25-34)

[1]Dallas Willard, *The Divine Conspiracy: Rediscovering Our Hidden Life in God* (San Francisco: HarperSanFrancisco, 1998), 45.

[2]Ibid., 259.

[3]Ibid., 145.

[4]Matthew 6:33, paraphrased in ibid., 212.

CHAPTER 12: RELYING ON THE KINGDOM, ILLUSTRATED (DANIEL 6)

[1]Edward J. Young, "Daniel," in *The New Bible Commentary*, 3rd ed., ed. E. Guthrie and J. A. Motyer (Grand Rapids: Eerdmans, 1970), 695.

[2]Ibid.

OPENNESS TO THE SPIRIT

[1]A. W. Tozer, *The Pursuit of God* (Camp Hill, PA: Christian Publications, 1982), 81-82.

[2]M. Robert Mulholland Jr., *Shaped by the Word* (Nashville: Upper Room Books, 2000), 43.

CHAPTER 13: THE HIDDEN YET POWERFUL KINGDOM OF GOD (MATTHEW 13:24-32, 36-40)

[1]Jan Johnson, *Invitation to the Jesus Life* (Colorado Springs, CO: Nav-Press, 2008), 163-64.

CHAPTER 14: THE HIDDEN YET POWERFUL KINGDOM OF GOD, ILLUSTRATED (2 KINGS 6:15-23)

[1]"Fire," in *International Standard Bible Encyclopedia*, vol. 2 (Grand Rapids: Eerdmans, 1939), 1112.

[2]Dallas Willard, *The Divine Conspiracy: Rediscovering Our Hidden Life in God* (San Francisco: HarperSanFrancisco, 1998), 69.

[3]*New Commentary on the Whole Bible: Old Testament Volume*, based on the classic commentary of Robert Jamieson, Andrew R. Fausset, and David Brown (Wheaton, IL: Tyndale House Publishers, 1990), comments on 2 Kings 6:17.

CHAPTER 15: THE GOOD AND PEACEABLE KINGDOM OF GOD (ISAIAH 11:1-9)

[1]Edward Hicks depicted this scene in his famous painting *The Peaceable Kingdom* (1826). www.worcesterart.org/collection/American/1934.65.html.

[2]*New Commentary on the Whole Bible: Old Testament Volume*, based on the classic commentary of Robert Jamieson, Andrew R. Fausset, and David Brown (Wheaton, IL: Tyndale House Publishers, 1990), comments on Isaiah 11:6, 7.

AM I HEARING GOD OR MAKING THINGS UP?

[1]E. Stanley Jones, *A Song of Ascents* (Nashville: Abingdon, 1979), 190.

[2]Dallas Willard, *Hearing God* (Downers Grove, IL: InterVarsity Press, 2012), 238.

CHAPTER 16: ABIDING IN CHRIST (JOHN 15:1-11)

[1]Andrew Murray, *Abide in Christ* (New Canaan, CT: Keats Publishing, 1973), vii.

[2]Richard Foster, *Celebration of Discipline* (San Francisco: Harper & Row, 1988), 30-31.

[3]Dallas Willard, *Renovation of the Heart* (Colorado Springs, CO: NavPress, 2002), 132.

[4]Rodney A. Whitacre, *John*, IVP New Testament Commentary (Downers Grove, IL: InterVarsity Press, 1999), 373.

[5]Murray, *Abide in Christ*, vii.

[6]Ibid., 2.

[7]Ibid., 18.

CHAPTER 17: FROM GANGSTER TO GIVER (LUKE 19:1-10)

[1]Kenneth E. Bailey, *Jesus Through Middle Eastern Eyes: Cultural Studies in the Gospels* (Downers Grove, IL: IVP Academic, 2008), 177.

WHEN YOUR MIND WANDERS

[1]Chester P. Michael and Marie C. Norrisey, *Prayer and Temperament* (Charlottesville, VA: The Open Door, 1991), 35.

CHAPTER 18: LETTING GO OF THE OLD SELF (COLOSSIANS 3:1-11)

[1]Dallas Willard, *Renovation of the Heart* (Colorado Springs, CO: NavPress, 2002), 33.

[2]"Scythians," in *International Standard Bible: Encyclopedia*, vol. 4 (Grand Rapids: Eerdmans, 1939), 2706.

[3]Dallas Willard, *The Spirit of the Disciplines* (San Francisco: Harper & Row, 1988), 36-37, 38.

[4]Dallas Willard, *The Divine Conspiracy: Rediscovering Our Hidden Life in God* (San Francisco: HarperSanFrancisco, 1998), 351.

[5]Ibid., 126.

[6]Willard, *Renovation of the Heart*, 102.

CHAPTER 19: EMBRACING THE NEW SELF (COLOSSIANS 3:12-17)

[1]Adam Clark in *The Bethany Parallel Commentary on the New Testament* (Minneapolis: Bethany House Publishers, 1963), 1195.

[2]Donald Guthrie, "Colossians," in *The New Bible Commentary*, 3rd ed., ed. E. Guthrie and J. A. Motyer (Grand Rapids: Eerdmans, 1970), 1150.

CHAPTER 20: DYING TO SELF (JOHN 13:1-14)

[1]Jan Johnson, *Invitation to the Jesus Life* (Colorado Springs, CO: Nav-Press, 2008), 188.

[2]Ibid., 192.

CHAPTER 21: FINDING COURAGE IN THE STORM (MARK 4:35-41)

[1]Richard Foster, *Celebration of Discipline* (San Francisco: Harper & Row, 1988), 30-31.

[2]You can find the painting at www.rembrandtpainting.net /rmbrndt_1620-35/christ_in_storm.htm.

[3]For a longer meditation using this painting, see Juliet Benner's excellent book *Contemplative Vision: A Guide to Christian Art and Prayer* (Downers Grove, IL: InterVarsity Press, 2011), 78-87.

DIVING BOARD LECTIO

[1]This phrase and several others in this section are taken from an email sent by Dallas Willard to Thomas Dervartanian on August 17, 2006. Used by permission.

CHAPTER 22: MOVING THROUGH A FEARFUL JOURNEY (PSALM 91)

[1]N. T. Wright, *Following Jesus* (Grand Rapids: Eerdmans, 1994), 66.

[2]Walter Brueggemann explains this in *The Message of the Psalms: A Theological Commentary* (Minneapolis: Augsburg, 1984), 156.

[3]Ibid., 157.

CHAPTER 24: MOVING FROM CYNICISM TO HOPE (PSALM 27)

[1]Dallas Willard, "Spirituality and Ministry," Fuller Seminary class (June 7, 2012).

[2]"yesha," James Strong, *The New Strong's Exhaustive Concordance of the Bible* (Nashville: Thomas Nelson Publishers, 2010), 61.

[3]"Salvation in the Old Testament," in *International Standard Bible Encyclopedia*, vol. 4 (Grand Rapids: Eerdmans, 1939), 2665. Salvation, then, takes countless forms—deliverance from natural plagues, from internal dissensions, from external enemies or from the subjugation of conquerors.

[4]Walter Brueggemann, *The Message of the Psalms* (Minneapolis: Augsburg, 1984), 140.

[5]Ibid., 152-57.

WHAT IF NOTHING COMES TO ME?

[1]Thelma Hall, *Too Deep for Words: Rediscovering Lectio Divina* (New York: Paulist Press, 1988), 32.

[2]Interview with Dallas Willard, July 31, 2002, Chatsworth, CA.

[3]"The Practice of Listening: An Interview with Madeleine L'Engle," *Crosspoints*, Summer 1997, 3.

CHAPTER 25: HEARING GOD IN THE MIDST OF DISCOURAGEMENT (1 KINGS 19:1-18)

[1]William Sanford La Sor, "1 and 2 Kings," in *The New Bible Commentary*, 3rd ed., ed. E. Guthrie and J. A. Motyer (Grand Rapids: Eerdmans, 1970), 345.

[2]Dallas Willard, *Hearing God: Developing a Conversational Relationship with God* (Downers Grove, IL: InterVarsity Press, 2012), 44.

[3]J. A. Thompson, *Handbook of Life in Bible Times* (Leicester, UK: InterVarsity Press, 1986), 22.

CHAPTER 26: BEING FREED FROM INFIRMITIES (LUKE 13:10-17)

[1]Tom Wright, *Luke for Everyone* (Louisville, KY: Westminster John Knox Press, 2004), 166.

CHAPTER 27: KNOWING THAT GOD HEARS ME (MARK 5:24-34)

[1]William Barclay, *The Daily Bible Study: The Gospel of Mark* (Philadelphia: Westminister Press, 1956), 128.

[2]William Barclay, *The Daily Bible Study: The Gospel of Luke* (Philadelphia: Westminister Press, 1956), 114.

[3]Alfred Edersheim, *The Life and Times of Jesus the Messiah* (Peabody, MA: Hendrickson Publishers, 1993), 428-29.

CHAPTER 28: ARE YOU WILLING TO BE HEALED? (JOHN 5:1-9)

[1]Frederic Louis Godet, *Commentary on John's Gospel* (Grand Rapids: Kregal Publications, 1978), 455.

CHAPTER 29: MOVING FROM MOURNING TO DANCING (PSALM 30)

[1]Jan Johnson, *Enjoying the Presence of God* (Colorado Springs, CO: NavPress, 1996), 112-13.

CHAPTER 30: RECEIVING JESUS' WORDS TO CAREGIVERS (MARK 9:14-29)

[1]Alfred Edersheim, *The Life and Times of Jesus the Messiah* (Peabody, MA: Hendrickson, 1993), 65.

CHAPTER 31: LOVING OTHERS IN TRUTH AND ACTION (JAMES 1:19-27)

[1]Veronica Zundel, ed., *Eerdmans' Book of Famous Prayers: A Treasury of Christian Prayers Through the Centuries* (Grand Rapids: Eerdmans, 1983), 99.

[2]Dallas Willard, *The Divine Conspiracy: Rediscovering Our Hidden Life in God* (San Francisco: HarperSanFrancisco, 1998), 145.

[3]Tom Wright, *Early Christian Letters for Everyone* (Louisville, KY: Westminster John Knox, 2011), 11.

[4]Ibid., 9.

[5]Ibid., 11.

CHAPTER 32: MOVING FROM SELF-ABSORPTION TO HUMILITY (PHILIPPIANS 2:1-16)

[1]Based on the meaning of Greek words and phrases as explained in Gerald F. Hawthorne, *Philippians*, Word Biblical Commentary (Waco, TX: Word Publishers, 1983), 68.

[2]William Barclay, *Daily Bible Study: The Letter to the Philippians* (Philadelphia: Westminister Press, 1959), 3-5.

CHAPTER 33: LOVING THE "STRANGER" (LUKE 10:25-37)

[1]Tom Wright, *Luke for Everyone* (Louisville, KY: Westminster John Knox, 2004), 127.

[2]Jan Johnson, *Growing Compassionate Kids* (Nashville: Upper Room Books, 2001), 41.

[3]Wright, *Luke for Everyone*, 126.

[4]Jan Johnson, *Invitation to the Jesus Life* (Colorado Springs, CO: NavPress, 2008), 70.

[5]Jesus liked to leave parables unfinished. Did the older brother of the prodigal son come in to the party (Luke 15:24-31)? Did the five foolish bridesmaids make it to the wedding (Matthew 25:1-13)? Did the workers who worked all day take their pay and leave or did they keep complaining (Matthew 20:1-16)? See Ken Bailey, *Jesus Through Middle Eastern Eyes: Cultural Studies in the Gospels* (Downers Grove, IL: IVP Academic, 2008), 273, 296, 357, 362.

[6]Ibid., 296.

[7]Dallas Willard defines *agapē* love as the "will to good or 'bene-volence.' We love something or someone when we promote their good for their own sake." Dallas Willard, *Renovation of the Heart* (Colorado Springs, CO: NavPress, 2002), 130.

CHAPTER 34: CHOOSING RELATIONSHIP OVER JUDGMENT (LUKE 6:36-38; MATTHEW 5:43-48)

[1]Tom Wright, *Luke for Everyone* (Louisville, KY: Westminster John Knox, 2004), 73.

[2]Dallas Willard defines *agapē* love as the "will to good or 'bene-volence.' We love something or someone when we promote their good for their own sake." Dallas Willard, *Renovation of the Heart* (Colorado Springs, CO: NavPress, 2002), 130.

CHAPTER 35: STEPPING OUT IN COMPASSION (LUKE 7:11-17)

[1]William Barclay, *Daily Bible Study: The Gospel of Luke* (Philadelphia: Westminister Press, 1956), 85.

²Tom Wright, *Luke for Everyone* (Louisville, KY: Westminster John Knox, 2004), 83.

³John Beck, "Widow," in *The Baker Illustrated Guide to Everyday Life in Bible Times* (Grand Rapids: Baker Books, 2013), 293.

⁴Wright, *Luke for Everyone*, 83.

⁵Ibid.

CHAPTER 36: COOPERATING WITH THE POWER OF GOD (EPHESIANS 3:14-21)

¹Richard Foster, *Celebration of Discipline* (San Francisco: Harper & Row, 1988), 30-31.

²Tom Wright, *Paul for Everyone: The Prison Letters* (Louisville, KY: Westminster John Knox, 2004), 39.

CHAPTER 37: RESPONDING TO THE PASSION GOD PUTS IN OUR HEARTS (NEHEMIAH 1–2)

¹V. Gilbert Beers, *The Victor Journey Through the Bible* (Wheaton, IL: Victor Books, 1996), 179, 182-83.

CHAPTER 38: RELATING TO GOD IN FAILURE (MATTHEW 14:22-33)

¹Tom Wright, *Matthew for Everyone, Part 1: Chapters 1–15* (Louisville, KY: Westminster John Knox, 2004), 189.

²"This miracle also was not a mere display of power, but . . . caused by their need." Alfred Edersheim, *The Life and Times of Jesus the Messiah* (Peabody, MA: Hendrickson, 1993), 473.

³Leslie Weatherhead, *The Transforming Friendship* (Nashville: Abingdon, 1977), 32-33.

⁴Wright, *Matthew for Everyone, Part 1*, 189.

⁵Dallas Willard, *The Divine Conspiracy: Rediscovering Our Hidden Life in God* (San Francisco: HarperSanFrancisco, 1998), 211.

⁶Jan Johnson, *Invitation to the Jesus Life* (Colorado Springs, CO: NavPress, 2008), 159.

CHAPTER 39: DRINKING THE CUP OF SUFFERING (MATTHEW 20:20-28)

[1]Oswald Chambers, *My Utmost for His Highest* (Westwood, NJ: Barbour and Company, 1963), 40.

[2]William Barclay, *The Gospel of Matthew: The Daily Study Bible*, vol. 2 (Philadelphia: Westminster Press, 1958), 255.

CHAPTER 40: DOING NOTHING ON MY OWN (PROVERBS 3:5-8)

[1]Dallas Willard, *Renovation of the Heart* (Colorado Springs, CO: Nav-Press, 2002), 33-35.

[2]Dallas Willard, *The Spirit of the Disciplines* (San Francisco: HarperSan-Francisco, 1988), 56.

[3]Andrew Murray, *Humility*, as paraphrased in Carlo Walth, *Humbling Guide: Andrew Murray's Humility Edited for the 21st Century Reader* (Mentoring Sacred Arts, 2012), 34.

[4]Andrew Murray, *The True Vine* (Chicago, IL: Moody Press, n.d.), 82.

HOW TO MEDITATE ON YOUR OWN

[1]E. Glenn Hinson, *Spiritual Preparation for Christian Leadership* (Nashville: Upper Room Books, 1999), 56.

[2]Dietrich Bonhoeffer, *Life Together* (New York: Harper & Row, 1954), 80-81.

formatio
TRADITION. EXPERIENCE.
TRANSFORMATION.

Formatio books from InterVarsity Press follow the rich tradition of the church in the journey of spiritual formation. These books are not merely about being informed, but about being transformed by Christ and conformed to his image. Formatio stands in InterVarsity Press's evangelical publishing tradition by integrating God's Word with spiritual practice and by prompting readers to move from inward change to outward witness. InterVarsity Press uses the chambered nautilus for Formatio, a symbol of spiritual formation because of its continual spiral journey outward as it moves from its center. We believe that each of us is made with a deep desire to be in God's presence. Formatio books help us to fulfill our deepest desires and to become our true selves in light of God's grace.